Jose Batista

Analysis of Random Fragment Profiles

Jose Batista

Analysis of Random Fragment Profiles

Detection of Structure-Activity Relationships and the Design of novel activity-directed Structural Descriptors

Südwestdeutscher Verlag für Hochschulschriften

Impressum/Imprint (nur für Deutschland/ only for Germany)
Bibliografische Information der Deutschen Nationalbibliothek: Die Deutsche Nationalbibliothek verzeichnet diese Publikation in der Deutschen Nationalbibliografie; detaillierte bibliografische Daten sind im Internet über http://dnb.d-nb.de abrufbar.

Alle in diesem Buch genannten Marken und Produktnamen unterliegen warenzeichen-, marken- oder patentrechtlichem Schutz bzw. sind Warenzeichen oder eingetragene Warenzeichen der jeweiligen Inhaber. Die Wiedergabe von Marken, Produktnamen, Gebrauchsnamen, Handelsnamen, Warenbezeichnungen u.s.w. in diesem Werk berechtigt auch ohne besondere Kennzeichnung nicht zu der Annahme, dass solche Namen im Sinne der Warenzeichen- und Markenschutzgesetzgebung als frei zu betrachten wären und daher von jedermann benutzt werden dürften.

Verlag: Südwestdeutscher Verlag für Hochschulschriften Aktiengesellschaft & Co. KG
Dudweiler Landstr. 99, 66123 Saarbrücken, Deutschland
Telefon +49 681 37 20 271-1, Telefax +49 681 37 20 271-0
Email: info@svh-verlag.de
Zugl.: Bonn, Rheinische Friedrich-Wilhelms-Universität, Dissertation, 2008

Herstellung in Deutschland:
Schaltungsdienst Lange o.H.G., Berlin
Books on Demand GmbH, Norderstedt
Reha GmbH, Saarbrücken
Amazon Distribution GmbH, Leipzig
ISBN: 978-3-8381-0171-2

Imprint (only for USA, GB)
Bibliographic information published by the Deutsche Nationalbibliothek: The Deutsche Nationalbibliothek lists this publication in the Deutsche Nationalbibliografie; detailed bibliographic data are available in the Internet at http://dnb.d-nb.de.

Any brand names and product names mentioned in this book are subject to trademark, brand or patent protection and are trademarks or registered trademarks of their respective holders. The use of brand names, product names, common names, trade names, product descriptions etc. even without a particular marking in this works is in no way to be construed to mean that such names may be regarded as unrestricted in respect of trademark and brand protection legislation and could thus be used by anyone.

Publisher: Südwestdeutscher Verlag für Hochschulschriften Aktiengesellschaft & Co. KG
Dudweiler Landstr. 99, 66123 Saarbrücken, Germany
Phone +49 681 37 20 271-1, Fax +49 681 37 20 271-0
Email: info@svh-verlag.de

Printed in the U.S.A.
Printed in the U.K. by (see last page)
ISBN: 978-3-8381-0171-2

Copyright © 2010 by the author and Südwestdeutscher Verlag für Hochschulschriften Aktiengesellschaft & Co. KG and licensors
All rights reserved. Saarbrücken 2010

Acknowledgments

I am grateful to my supervisor Prof. Dr. Jürgen Bajorath for his guidance and his support not only during the work on this project. I would like to thank Prof. Dr. Christa Müller for her willingness to be co-referent of my PhD-thesis. I also want to thank Eugen Lounkine and Jens Auer for numerous and fruitful discussions. Thank you for all my colleagues here at the B-IT in Bonn for the pleasant working atmosphere and countless good moments. Finally, I like to hug Britta Schürmann for all she has done for me and my family.

Contents

1 Introduction   1

2 Methodology   9
    2.1 Molecular Graph Representations 9
         2.1.1 Connection Tables 10
         2.1.2 Linear Notation 11
    2.2 MolBlaster Fragmentation 11
         2.2.1 Histogram Representation 13
         2.2.2 Complexity Independent Fragmentation 15
    2.3 Information Content of Histograms 15
         2.3.1 Shannon Entropy 15
         2.3.2 Differential Shannon Entropy 16

3 Similarity Assessment   19
    3.1 Detection of Structural Resemblance 20
         3.1.1 Preferred Fragmentation Levels 22
         3.1.2 Evaluation 23
    3.2 Detection of Structure-Activity Relationships 25
         3.2.1 Methodology 26
         3.2.2 Evaluation in Similarity Search Trials 30
    3.3 Summary and Conclusions 36

4 Mining Fragment Profiles   37
    4.1 Mining of Random Fragment Profiles 37
         4.1.1 Composition of Fragment Profiles 37
    4.2 Detection of Fragment Hierarchies 40
         4.2.1 Methodology for Mining Dependency Relationships 41
         4.2.2 Analysis of Fragment Dependency Hierarchies 44
    4.3 Similarity Searching Using Fragment Hierarchies 49
         4.3.1 Methodology for Similarity Searching 50
         4.3.2 Analysis of Similarity Search Results 51
    4.4 Conclusion 55

5	**Distribution and Origin of ACCS**		**57**
	5.1	Distribution of ACCS	57
		5.1.1 Methodology	57
		5.1.2 Evaluation	58
	5.2	Origin of ACCS	60
		5.2.1 Molecular Mapping	60
		5.2.2 Observations for Molecular Mapping	63
		5.2.3 Structural Meaning of Fragment Hierarchies	63
	5.3	Summary and Conclusions	64
6	**Summary and Conclusions**		**65**
A	**Software and Databases**		**69**
B	**Mining Frequently Occurring Fragments**		**71**
C	**Screening Dataset**		**73**
D	**Class-Unique ACCS combinations**		**75**
	Bibliography		**79**

Chapter 1

Introduction

Substructures of synthetic compounds and dictionaries of molecular fragments are widely used tools in many computational applications in the area of medicinal chemistry, drug design, and chemoinformatics [1]. They are often preferred descriptors for similarity searching, compound classification, diversity design, or the analysis of structure-activity relationships; for several reasons. Fragment descriptors are simplistic in their design because they utilize only information provided by 2D molecular graphs and their application is computationally highly efficient. Moreover, they are chemically intuitive and can be much easier appreciated than many other more complex mathematical models of chemical structures and properties. Most importantly, given the simplicity and intuitive nature of their design, substructures and fragment descriptors are surprisingly powerful in analyzing and predicting structure-activity relationships. This is very likely the case because these types of descriptors implicitly capture much chemical information [2; 3]. The often observed high performance of fragment descriptors also implies that many determinants of the biological activity of small molecules can already be deduced from 2D molecular graph representations. This is an attractive concept for medicinal chemists who are primarily trained on such molecular representations.

The terms substructures and fragments are often synonymously used and there are no generally accepted definitions that would clearly distinguish between them. However, substructures are often understood as chemically interpretable moieties such as, for example, intact rings, parts of rings, or amide bond units, whereas fragments can be rather generic structural units, down to the level of single atoms. For the purpose of present thesis, no further distinction between substructures and fragments are made. Here, a functional group in a molecule such as an amino or hydroxyl group might either be considered a substructure or a fragment.

A hallmark of current state-of-the-art fragment descriptors is that they are commonly generated in a controlled and well-defined manner. This is accomplished through the application of systematic and/or hierarchical molecular fragmentation schemes that are supported by chemical knowledge and intuition or by taking synthetic or retrosynthetic criteria into account. Only recently, random approaches have been introduced to generate fragment sources allowing the identification of substructures that are associated with different biological activities.

Historical Overview

The introduction of molecular fragments as tools for chemical analysis dates back to the 1950s when fragment collections were generated on the basis of topological criteria, i.e. by adding layers of bonded atoms to pre-selected central atoms [4]. These so-called *atom-centered* fragments were originally applied to estimate physical properties of synthetic molecules such as, for example, P(o/w), the octanol-water partition coefficient. The distribution of atom-centered fragments in chemical databases was first studied in the early 1970s [5] and later on fragment descriptors were used to associate small molecules with biological activities [6; 7]. During the same decade, methods were introduced for the systematic generation of sets of atom- or *bond-centered* fragments that occur with a certain frequency (e.g. equal frequency) in a database [8; 9]. The most efficient approaches were based on the Morgan algorithm published in 1965 [10] and the resulting fragments were used as so-called *screen sets* for database searching [8; 9]. During the 1970s, atom- and bond-centered fragments were also encoded as bit strings for the first time [11; 12], and these fingerprint representations of molecular structures have continued to be one of the most widely used descriptor formats for chemical similarity searching to this date.

Fingerprint searching became already popular during the 1980s, for example, through the works of Carhart et al. [13] and Willett [14], due to the notion that structural resemblance between pairs of molecules can simply be determined by counting the number of common fragments. As a consequence various similarity metrics have been introduced to quantitatively determine fingerprint overlap as a measure of molecular similarity [14]. Today the most popular dictionaries of fragments for fingerprint similarity searching include a set of 166 publicly available MACCS structural keys [15] or the BCI standard dictionary with 1 052 fragments [16].

Principal Approaches to Fragment Design

Fragment descriptors continue to be very widely used and, accordingly, different types of fragments have been introduced, in part for specialized applications. Contemporary strategies to fragment design and generation can essentially be divided into three major categories; knowledge-based, systematic and hierarchical, and synthetically-oriented approaches.

Knowledge-based methods make use of chemical and pharmaceutical expertise to design substructures. For example, knowledge-based dictionaries have been established to predict pharmacological properties of bioactive substances [17] or the removal of compounds with reactive or toxic fragments from screening sets [18; 19]. Another example of knowledge-based design is the definition of privileged substructures that are recurrent in compounds with activity against members of therapeutic target families, e.g. G-protein coupled receptors [20; 21] or protein kinases [22; 23]. Furthermore, substructures are often designed on the basis of known active molecules for the generation of target-focused combinatorial libraries [24] or for diversity-oriented synthesis [25] in order to preferentially explore pharmaceutically relevant regions of chemical space. These substructures are typically called *scaffolds* because they

CHAPTER 1. INTRODUCTION 3

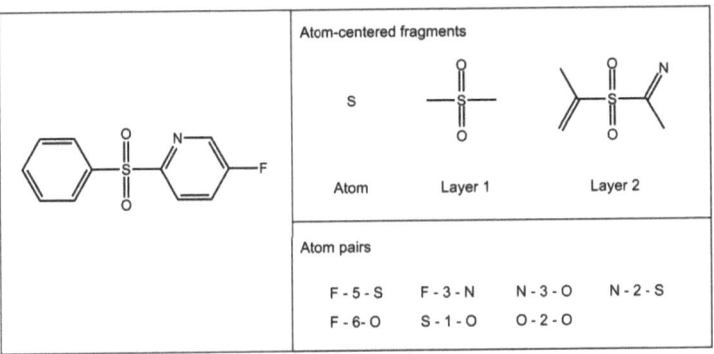

Fig. 1.1: Atom-centered fragments and atom pairs. For the molecule on the left, examples of atom-centered fragments and atom pairs are given. The upper right panel shows atom-centered fragments for the sulfur atom up to bond layer 2. The lower right panel shows atom pairs for the heteroatoms.

represent molecular building blocks that are subjected to chemical modification.

Systematic approaches to generate atom- and bond-centered fragments were one of the origins of this field, as discussed above. Exemplary atom-centered fragments are illustrated in Figure 1.1. In the analysis of such fragments, it was often attempted to systematically identify fragments that are distributed with comparable frequency in databases. Early efforts to derive atom- and bond-centered fragments provided the basis for the design of fingerprints that capture strings of layered atom environments [26; 27]. Currently these fingerprints are among the state-of-the-art similarity search tools. *Atom pairs* represent another pioneering development of fragment-type descriptors that were systematically derived following topological criteria [13]. These descriptors describe triplets of the form AT_i-$Dist_{ij}$-AT_j, where $Dist_{ij}$ is the length of the shortest bond path between an atom of type AT_i and another of type AT_j. Further refined atom types encode the element as well as the number of attached non-hydrogen atoms and the number of π-electrons [28]. An example is provided in the lower panel of Figure 1.1. Going beyond these topology-oriented approaches for systematic fragment generation, hierarchical methods have been introduced by Bemis and Murcko [29; 30] to reduce 2D molecular graphs to structural elements that are most relevant for molecular design and the study of structure-activity relationships. The hierarchical approach divides molecules into ring structures, linkers and side chains that are systematically isolated, as shown in Figure 1.2. Different levels of abstraction can be applied to represent compounds. In the context of hierarchical methods, heteroatom-containing core structures without side chains (functional groups) are regarded as scaffolds, while molecular frameworks are obtained from these scaffolds by replacing all heteroatoms with carbon atoms.

Synthetic criteria are also used to guide fragment design. One application is the selection of core structures for diversity-oriented synthesis efforts, because such structures need to be synthetically accessible and must have the potential for systematic chemical modification at pre-selected points of diversification. Moreover, retrosynthetic fragmentation schemes have

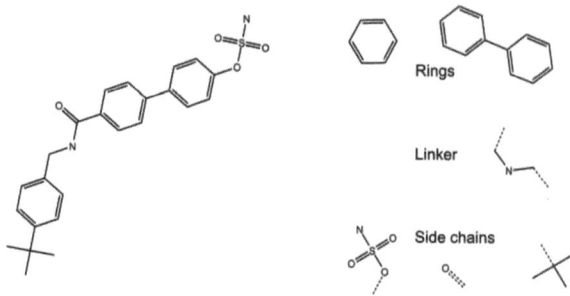

Fig. 1.2: Hierarchical fragmentation scheme. The figure shows the fragmentation of an exemplary molecule into a ring system, a linker, and side chains. Dashed bonds are cleaved during fragmentation and are not part of the fragments.

been developed in order to generate building blocks for library design [31; 32]. In principle, such substructures are obtained by breaking bonds in molecules that are formed by cataloged chemical reactions [32; 33]. The basic idea underlying retrosynthetic approaches is that the resulting fragments can be chemically re-combined in different ways. A pioneering effort in this area has been the introduction of RECAP [34] that defines 11 chemical bond types based on reaction information where cleavage can occur, as shown in Figure 1.3. The ability of recombination is highly relevant, for example, to synthesize a spectrum of novel compounds that are tailored towards the requirements of biological screening programs [35].

The generation of popular dictionaries of structural keys, as mentioned above, typically combines systematic and knowledge-based design elements. For example, fragment sets can be

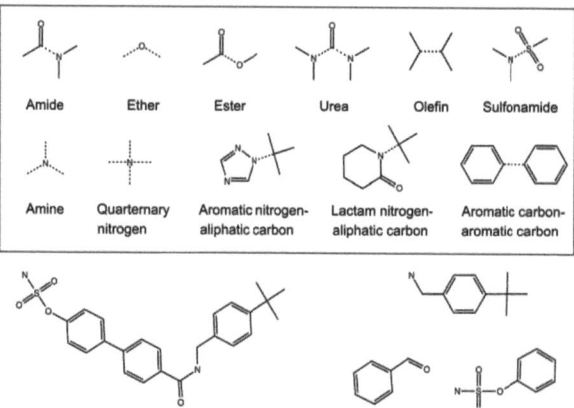

Fig. 1.3: RECAP bond types. The upper panel shows the eleven types of cleavable bonds that constitute the RECAP fragmentation scheme (indicated by dashed lines). The resulting fragments can be recombined to form new compounds because the fragmentation scheme reflects common chemical reactions. The lower part illustrates RECAP fragmentation for an exemplary compound. The molecule is cleaved at the amide and biphenyl bonds.

systematically extracted from compound collections, manually modified, or generalized (similar to molecular frameworks) [16]. Visual inspection and interactive curation of fragment sets further ensure high quality. In addition, fragment dictionaries can be redesigned for drug discovery applications by analyzing the distribution of fragments in pharmaceutically-relevant compounds and adjusting the composition of fragment sets [36].

An intrinsic feature of the introduced strategies is that generated substructures focus on specific chemical features of the represented molecule set. Therefore, different 2D descriptors perform well for varying applications. Because nowadays a large number of 2D descriptors are available [37], finding descriptor combinations suitable for specific chemoinformatics applications is often a crucial step, and much emphasis has been put on trying to rationalize this process [38; 39; 40]. Besides the major categories of fragment methods there are only a limited number that depart from systematic and knowledge-based strategies but rather focus on random fragment generation. One example is the Brownian approach to fragment sampling, as discussed in the following section.

Brownian Processing and Substructure Generation

Graham et al. [41] assessed the information content of organic molecules based on so-called tape recordings of random walks through molecular graphs. In their studies molecules are taken as devices carrying information about chemical properties like mass, charge, energy and others. The information is quantified through sensing of the molecular substructures, thereby imitating the recognition of the compounds during chemical reactions.

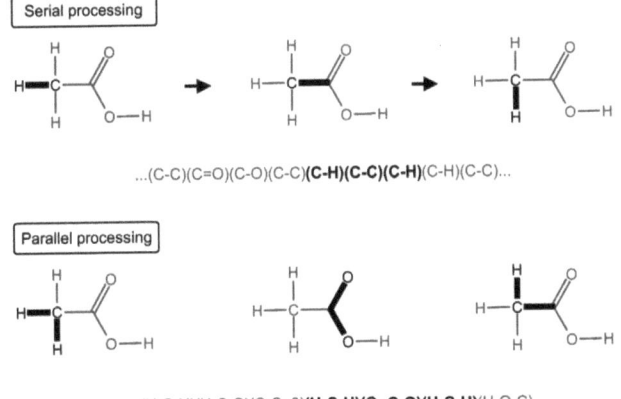

Fig. 1.4: Brownian processing. Exemplary random walks through a molecule and the corresponding tape recordings are illustrated. Visited pairs of atoms are indicated through bold bonds, which are also emphasized in the tape recordings. The upper part of the figure shows a serial random walk, while the lower part demonstrates an example of a parallel walk producing code units of length two.

A step in this so-called Brownian processing is defined by a bonded atom pair as well as the bond order and proceeds by randomly selecting the next bond connecting a current atom to a neighbor. The generation of tape recordings can be performed in serial or parallel order and is illustrated in Figure 1.4. In serial processing, each visited atom pair is stored as a code unit while for parallel processing code units of a given length are extracted. These units represent substructures of a compound and contain information about topological pathways. The chemical information content of molecules can then be evaluated by analyzing the frequency with which substructures up to a certain length (e.g. atom pairs, triplets, etc.) occur or by analyzing to what extent they are correlated to each other. Brownian processing was used by Graham and co-workers for the evaluation of organic compounds and their chemical properties. In their study they demonstrated that the information content of a molecule is closely linked to its chemical properties [42; 43]. This approach is only distantly related to a systematic exploration of connectivity pathways through a molecule for the design of 2D fingerprints or the generation of structural descriptors.

Research topics

The fundamental aim of this project was to explore whether randomly generated fragment populations could be successfully used for the detection of structure-activity relationships. Our motivation was to design a similarity method to systematically identify highly discriminatory substructures for a class of active compounds without depending on a predefined molecular organization scheme like the methods discussed above. The availability of such activity class-specific substructures would provide new opportunities for descriptor design and selection for particular applications, which often represent challenging tasks [2].

In this thesis a conceptually different approach for the generation and analysis of randomly generated fragment populations is introduced. Fragment populations are generated by random deletion of bonds in molecules and sampling of resulting substructures. This approach enables the evaluation and comparison of individual fragments and therefore departs from the design of tape recordings during Brownian processing. The thesis focuses on three central questions in order to analyze randomly generated fragment populations in detail.

Question 1: Can randomly generated fragments be used for the assessment of molecular similarity relationships?

The first step evaluates whether random fragment populations encode sufficient structural information for the assessment of structural resemblance between pairs of compounds. For this purpose the design of an applicable similarity metric is required to enable quantitative evaluation of fragment populations. In a subsequent step the applicability of randomly generated fragments for the detection of structure-activity relationships is analyzed. Therefore it is necessary to generate and analyze a fragment profile that yields structural information for a set of active compounds. For both approaches, the ability to evaluate molecular similarity relationships is compared to other state-of-the-art methods.

Question 2: Can signature substructures be identified from randomly generated fragment profiles that are characteristic for individual activity classes?

To answer this question randomly generated fragment profiles are analyzed at a molecular level of detail. Individual substructures of a fragment profile are related to each other whenever they are derived from the same molecule(s). The challenge is to clarify in which way randomly generated fragments are associated with each other and to formalize these relationships. One aspect of this question is to what extent individual fragments can be associated with the biological activity of their parent molecules. The intention is to identify activity-class characteristic fragments and eliminate non-specific substructures from a fragment profile. A second aspect is to analyze the potential of fragments to represent other substructures. This would reduce randomly generated fragment profiles to a minimum number of substructures that display structural information required to characterize individual compound sets.

Question 3: How can the predictive utility of randomly generated fragments be rationalized?

Answering this question provides insights into the discriminatory power of fragment signature sets. For this purpose the occurrence of class-specific fragments in sets of active and inactive compounds is studied. Furthermore, the structural meaning of small signature sets in parent compounds is analyzed.

Outline of the thesis

Chapter 2 represents the methodological part of this thesis. Beginning with an overview of molecular graph representations, the design of the developed random fragmentation scheme *MolBlaster* is reported. Then the representation of randomly generated fragment populations as histograms is explained. This enables the quantitative evaluation of the information content of fragment populations by newly introduced entropic metrics.

Chapter 3 focus on the first question under Research Topics. It provides evidence that randomly generated fragment populations can be successfully used for the detection of similarity relationships. First it is demonstrated that structural resemblance between compounds can be correctly reproduced using entropic metrics. Subsequently, fragment profiles of a set of active compounds are generated through classification of fragments according to their class-specific information content. The potential of information-rich fragments for detecting structure-activity relationships is demonstrated.

Chapter 4 discusses the second question under Research Topics. It reports a hierarchical organization of randomly generated fragment profiles that is based on conditional probabilities of fragment co-occurrence for diverse molecules. Multiple sets of compounds with different biological activity are used in order to identify subgraphs of Activity-Class Characteristic Substructures (ACCS) from these hierarchies. Based on the hierarchical organization of ACCS it is demonstrated by virtual screening trials that only a small number of fragments are required to detect structure-activity relationships.

Chapter 5 addresses the final question. To analyze the distribution of ACCS within active and background database compounds the occurrence of single fragments and fragment combinations in these sets is monitored. The analysis reveals that ACCS are rarely found in database compounds and that combinations of ACCS become signatures of the activity classes. In a second step the source of ACCS is studied. It is found that relatively small regions in parent molecules that contain recurrent structural patterns are the origin of ACCS.

Finally, *Chapter 6* summarizes the results.

Chapter 2

Methodology

A principal aim of this thesis is to analyze whether randomly generated molecular fragment populations can be used for detection of molecular similarity relationships. Therefore, some fundamental methodological problems have to be solved. First and foremost, an adequate fragmentation scheme is required that subjects diverse molecules to an extensive random fragmentation. Furthermore, generated fragment populations must be recorded in an accessible format in order to extract structural information. Moreover, a mathematical formalism is required to systematically evaluate the information content of fragment populations.
In this chapter, the most relevant concepts and methods are introduced. In Section 2.1 an overview of 2D molecular graph representations and applied formats is given. This is essential for the introduction of the random fragmentation approach termed MolBlaster[44] in Section 2.2. Critical parameters of the MolBlaster process and their effects on fragment profiles are discussed. In Subsection 2.2.1 the representation of fragment profiles as histograms is illustrated. It is shown that different compounds generate characteristic fragment populations, dependent on the size and topology of their molecular graphs. These topological differences between compounds can bias the evaluation of fragment populations for the detection of structural resemblance. Therefore a modification of the MolBlaster procedure is introduced in Subsection 2.2.2 that produces comparable fragment populations irrespective of the chemical complexity of studied compound sets. Finally, Section 2.3 gives an overview of the Shannon entropy concept and its applications. The introduced entropic methods are used to extract and quantify the information content encoded in histograms of fragment populations in order to systematically evaluate molecular similarity relationships.

2.1 Molecular Graph Representations

Chemical structures are usually stored in databases as 2D molecular graphs, due to their simple design and universal utility for relevant applications. Despite their low complexity, 2D graph representations have been successfully used for the detection of molecular similarity relationships, thereby often achieving better results than representations of higher complexity [2].

Generally, a graph is an abstract structure that consists of nodes connected by edges. In molecular graphs, the nodes correspond to atoms and the edges to bonds. Consequently, a graph represents the *topology* of a molecule, i.e. the way the atoms are connected. Hence, many approaches for well-known graph theoretical problems can be used for chemoinformatics applications. For example, to check if two molecules are equal, irrespective of their orientation, one can use algorithms for *graph isomorphism* [45; 46]. Further, *subgraph matching* methods help to decide whether or not a given substructure can be found within a molecule [47; 48].

2.1.1 Connection Tables

A common way to store and process molecular graphs on a computer is to encode them as a *connection table* that essentially consists of an *atom list* and a *bond list*. The atom list specifies in sequential order the atoms of the molecule, while the bond list specifies the connections between them as pairs of bonded atoms. A simple example of a connection table is given in Figure 2.1. This format, developed by MDL Information Systems [49], offers additional information about the 3D coordinates of the atoms. More detailed information such as the hybridization state of each atom can also be included in the connection table. Hydrogen atoms might only be implicitly included in a *hydrogen-suppressed* connectivity table. This reduction does not represent a loss of information because hydrogen atoms can be derived assuming standard valences for listed atoms. Also, the aromaticity of bonds can be supposed in connectivity tables as shown in Figure 2.1. Aromatic structures are then represented as tautomers, from which aromaticity can be deduced.

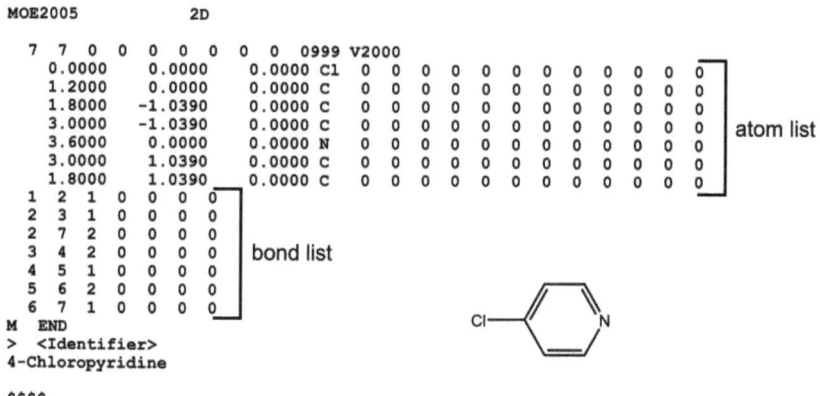

Fig. 2.1: Exemplary connection table. For the small molecule in the lower part of the figure a corresponding connection table is shown. The first part consists of the atom list specifying the atoms in sequential order. Additional information (e.g. 3D coordinates) are listed. The second part is composed by the bond list, which describes a set of bonded atom pairs and provides further information (e.g. the bond order). A closer look at the bond list shows that the chlorine atom (sequence number 1) is connected to the carbon atom with sequence number 2 through a single bond. The nitrogen atom (sequence number 5) is connected to two other carbon atoms, in one case through a double bond.

2.1.2 Linear Notation

An alternative way to encode molecular graphs is by means of a *linear notation*, which utilizes alphanumeric characters to encode a molecular structure. These notations are more compact than connectivity tables and thus particularly useful for storing and processing large numbers of molecules. A widely used linear notation is SMILES [50], that is hydrogen-suppressed and represents atoms by their atomic symbols. General concepts about SMILES are illustrated in Figure 2.2. Aromaticity is indicated by lower case letters, while upper case letters are used for aliphatic atoms. Bond orders of higher degree are specified using special symbols, e.g. "=" for double bonds and "#" for triple bonds; single and aromatic bonds are usually not explicitly represented. Linear encoding of ring systems is performed by breaking one bond of each ring. The presence of rings is then indicated by appending a unique integer identifier to the two atoms of the broken bond. Branching points of a molecule are represented using parentheses; all atoms within a pair belong to the same branch. If necessary, branches are nested.

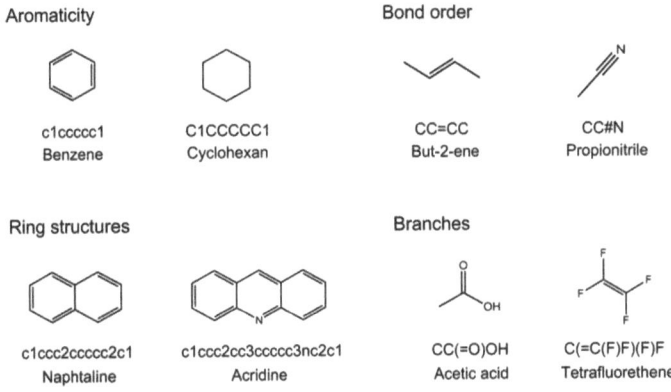

Fig. 2.2: **Illustration of SMILES strings.** Shown are exemplary realizations of the most relevant SMILES concepts. For each structure the corresponding SMILES string and the trivial name is provided.

2.2 MolBlaster Fragmentation

Molecular fragmentation is achieved by random deletion of rows in connectivity tables of hydrogen-suppressed 2D graph representations. This process corresponds to randomly breaking bonds in a molecule and is illustrated in Figure 2.3. In order to obtain a significant number of diverse fragments this step is repeated many times. The number of bond deletions per iteration step is kept constant and the range of permitted random values is predetermined for the compound set considered for fragmentation. It corresponds to the number of rows for the molecule with the largest bond list. This ensures that all bonds of the molecule are deleted with the same probability. If a random number falls outside the range for a smaller structure, no deletion is carried out. From the reduced connectivity tables, SMILES strings of molecular

2.2. MOLBLASTER FRAGMENTATION

```
MOE2005              2D

 7  5  0  0  0  0  0  0  0  0999 V2000
    1.2000   -1.0000    0.0000 Cl  0  0  0  0  0  0  0  0  0  0  0  0
    1.2000   -2.2000    0.0000 C   0  0  0  0  0  0  0  0  0  0  0  0
    2.2390   -2.8000    0.0000 C   0  0  0  0  0  0  0  0  0  0  0  0
    0.0000    0.0000    0.0000 C   0  0  0  0  0  0  0  0  0  0  0  0
    1.2000    0.0000    0.0000 N   0  0  0  0  0  0  0  0  0  0  0  0
    2.4000    0.0000    0.0000 C   0  0  0  0  0  0  0  0  0  0  0  0
    0.1610   -2.8000    0.0000 C   0  0  0  0  0  0  0  0  0  0  0  0
  1  2  1  0  0  0  0
  2  3  1  0  0  0  0
  2  7  2  0  0  0  0
  4  5  1  0  0  0  0
  5  6  2  0  0  0  0
M  END
>  <Identifier>
4-Chloropyridine fragmented

$$$$
```

Fig. 2.3: Exemplary fragmentation step. The molecule reported in Figure 2.1 is cleaved through deletion of the randomly selected lines 4 and 7 in the corresponding bond list. Deletion of these lines results in a new connectivity table encoding two molecular fragments.

fragments are exported for fragment sampling, as shown in Figure 2.4. Connectivity tables for test compounds are calculated with the Molecular Operating Environment (MOE)[1] and rows are selected for deletion with a uniform random number generator. The MolBlaster approach was implemented in the Perl scripting language.

In principle, compound fragmentation depends on two parameters. First the maximum number of permitted bond deletions per iteration and second the total number of iterations. The general influence of the parameters on the composition of fragment population is analyzed in the following.

Number of Bond Deletions

The number of bond deletions per step affects the average size and length of the resulting fragments and thus the composition of the fragment population. If the selected parameter value is small, the generated fragments will be large on average and contain much of the structural information provided by the molecular graph. This might be disadvantageous for the detection of similarity relationships, because large fragments are mainly specific for their parent molecules. On the other hand, if there are too many deletions, the generated fragments are small in size and generic in shape. Thus fragmentation parameters must be carefully determined, because they strongly influence the information content of a fragment profile.

Number of Iterations

The number of iterations controls the total number of diverse fragments that are generated and the frequency of occurrence of each fragment. If the value of the parameter is low, the number of diverse fragments in the profile is low, too. This results in an coarse and unspecific fragment

---
[1]Software tools used throughout the thesis are described in Appendix A.

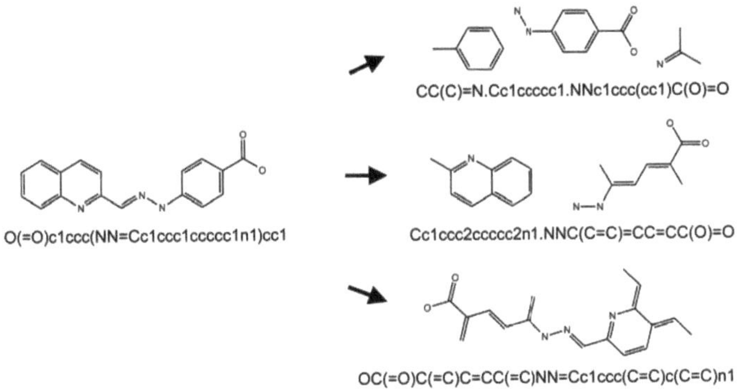

CHAPTER 2. METHODOLOGY																																			13

CC(C)=N.Cc1ccccc1.NNc1ccc(cc1)C(O)=O

O(=O)c1ccc(NN=Cc1ccc1ccccc1n1)cc1

Cc1ccc2ccccc2n1.NNC(C=C)=CC=CC(O)=O

OC(=O)C(=C)C=CC(=C)NN=Cc1ccc(C=C)c(C=C)n1

Fig. 2.4: Fragment representations. Shown are fragment sets of increasing size with corresponding SMILES string representations produced in different deletion steps. Unconnected structures within a SMILES string are indicated by a dot.

profile that covers only a small fraction of all possible molecular substructures. In contrast, if the number of iterations is too high, the fragmentation process will mainly generate redundant information. Thus, computational cost increases without a significant gain of structural information.

2.2.1 Histogram Representation

In order to monitor the fragment populations of molecules they are displayed in histograms. Here, each data point corresponds to a fragment and reports its occurrence frequency within the population. Figure 2.5 illustrates the features of fragment populations and their histogram representations for the compounds 1-octylphenanthrene and 2-phenylphenanthrene. Both compounds are derived from phenanthrene, an aromatic hydrocarbon composed of three fused benzene rings. The molecules only differ in their moieties connected to this scaffold. For 1-octylphenanthrene the substituent is octane, an aliphatic chain, whereas for 2-phenylphenanthrene it is benzene, an aromatic ring. Both molecules are fragmented using MolBlaster, with 5 bond deletions per step.

For 1-octylphenanthrene small fragments up to a length of 8 atoms show low diversity, but hold the largest portion of the population. This can be rationalized considering that only a single bond deletion is required to separate an alkane (aliphatic chain) from the molecule, which is very likely to occur. Highest diversity is observed for mid-size fragments (between 9 and 15 atoms), with a peak at 14 atoms. These structures are mostly generated through the cleavage of the phenanthrene scaffold. To split the ring system into distinct parts at least two deletions of appropriate bonds are required. Furthermore, the phenanthrene scaffold can tolerate 3 bond deletions without being reduced to a fragment of less than 14 atoms. Hence, phenanthrene is more resistant against decomposition. A larger number of different bond deletion combinations can be carried out, yielding a larger set of diverse fragments. For large fragments (more than

15 atoms) the diversity and frequency of occurrence decreases.

The analogue 2-phenylphenanthrene contains an additional ring instead of the aliphatic substituent and the increased ring content leads to the generation of larger fragments. Furthermore, the fragment distribution is more balanced than for the aliphatic phenanthrene derivative. The reason is that the benzene ring is more resistant against decomposition, which hinders the generation of small fragments. For 2-phenylphenanthrene the most frequent fragments consist of six atoms. These fragments are typically derived from the benzene ring because here only one bond deletion is required. To further reduce benzene to fragments with less than 6 atoms, at least two other bond deletions must occur.

The example illustrates that compounds of different topology produce different fragment populations. Even for closely related molecules such as phenanthrene analogues the fragment distributions differ. The conclusion is that fragment profiles are sensitive to characteristic molecular information, such as size and graph connectivity, and capable of differentiating between molecules having similar core structures.

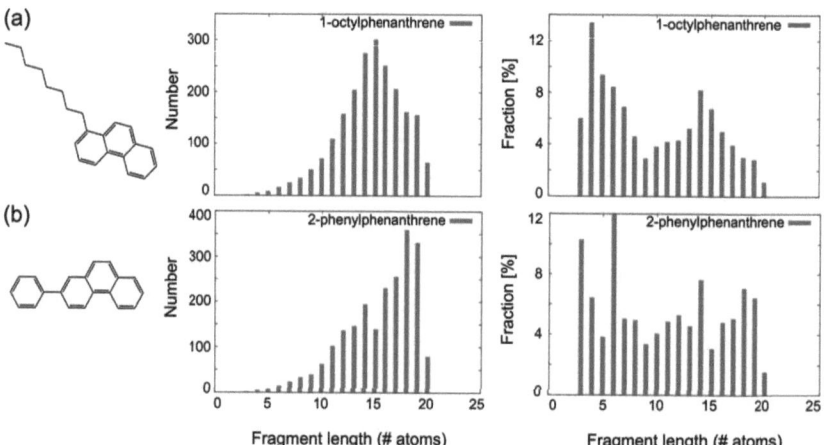

Fig. 2.5: **Fragment populations.** Shown are histogram representations of fragment populations generated from two molecules, permitting five bond deletions per step in calculations with 3 000 iterations: (a) 1-octylphenanthrene and (b) 2-phenylphenanthrene. The histograms on the left reflect the diversity of fragments of equal length. Here *Number* reports the count of unique (structurally distinct) fragments of equal size produced during the fragmentation process. The histograms on the right show the variation of fragment length within the fragment population. *Fraction* gives the percentage of fragments having a specific length of the total fragment population. In these calculations, multiple copies of the same fragments are taken into account. Fragments with one or two atoms were omitted from the profiles since they do not offer much structural information about their molecules.

2.2.2 Complexity Independent Fragmentation

Due to the differences in size and topology of molecules, fragmentation parameters that produce most representative populations can vary between distinct compound sets. Thus, it is very likely that a constant number of permitted deletions per iteration step will not produce fragment profiles that sufficiently account for structural differences between distinct compound classes. For the systematic analysis of structure-activity relationships a generally applicable approach is required that produces fragment populations of maximal information content irrespective of the topology and size of the molecules. Therefore, a modification of the MolBlaster fragmentation is introduced [51]. The number of permitted bond deletions during each iteration is randomized in order to balance the fragment generation for molecules having different degrees of complexity. It is expected that a significant number of diverse fragments with varying size is generated, enabling an adequate characterization of the compounds. Additionally, since all compounds are subjected to the same fragmentation procedure, the generated fragment profiles can be compared without further normalization.

2.3 Information Content of Histograms

In order to evaluate fragment populations of diverse compounds the populations are encoded as histograms, which is a common way to represent feature value distributions. The information content of a histogram can be determined using the Shannon entropy concept that has a long history. In a first publication in 1948 [52] Shannon studied the transmissions of messages from an information source over a noisy channel. Therefore he developed a theoretical communication model with an abstract information sender and receptor and hypothetical messages that consist of a set of symbols occurring with a certain frequency. Through the addition of redundant symbols it is possible to protect messages against information loss. In order to determine the amount of data that is required to account for the original message at the receptor, Shannon introduced the concept of *information entropy*, a quantitative measure of the information content of messages, i.e. data distributions. This seminal paper established information theory as a research area on its own. The concept of molecular information content was introduced in 1953 [53] and later in the 1970s the Shannon entropy was applied in the context of molecular graph theory [54]. Subsequently, this concept was also applied in computational chemistry [55; 56; 57].

2.3.1 Shannon Entropy

Briefly, Shannon entropy (SE) quantifies the information content in a data distribution as the minimal number of bits required to encode the information in binary format. It is defined as:

$$\text{SE} = -\sum_i p_i \log_2(p_i) \qquad (2.1)$$

where p_i is the probability of a data point i to occur within the data distribution. For the purposes of this thesis, a data point is equivalent to a molecular fragment. The probability is calculated as $p_i = c_i/total\_counts$, where c_i corresponds to the occurrence frequency of the specific fragment and $total\_counts = \sum_i c_i$ to the sum of all frequencies.

The Shannon entropy is maximal when the data is evenly distributed over all histogram bins. In this case the SE value is equal to the binary logarithm of the number of histogram bins utilized. Consequently the SE value is dependent on the number of data points used in the histograms and therefore the information content of data distributions of varying size cannot be compared directly. This dependence can be avoided by calculating the scaled Shannon entropy (sSE):

$$\text{sSE} = -\sum_i p_i \log_n(p_i) \qquad (2.2)$$

where n is the number of histogram bins (fragments). Then, independent of the number of bins (fragments), the calculated sSE lies within the range [0; 1], making the information content of diverse data distributions (fragment populations) comparable.

2.3.2 Differential Shannon Entropy

The Shannon entropy is a reasonable metric to determine whether a fragment population has a higher information content than another. This value does not ascertain the similarity between two profiles. An appropriate measure for this purpose is the Differential Shannon entropy (DSE) [58]. This metric quantifies differences in information content and variance for two feature value distributions. Primarily, DSE is designed to predict the degree to which descriptor distributions complement or duplicate information contained in large compound sets. It is defined as:

$$\text{DSE} = \text{SE}_{AB} - \left(\frac{\text{SE}_A + \text{SE}_B}{2}\right). \qquad (2.3)$$

SE_A and SE_B are the SE values for two different data distributions, or in this case, the fragment histograms of two molecules A and B. SE_{AB} refers to the Shannon entropy calculated from the combined histogram, reflecting the distribution of the merged fragment populations derived from both molecules. Thus, a non-zero DSE value represents an increase or decrease in data variability due to synergies in information content between the individual data distributions. In other words, the larger the absolute DSE value, the more distinct the individual data distributions. In Figure 2.6 some hypothetical data distributions are used to illustrate the significance of DSE values.

In order to apply the DSE metric as a similarity measure of fragment histograms, a scaled version of the metric must be deployed in analogy to sSE. Furthermore, differences between

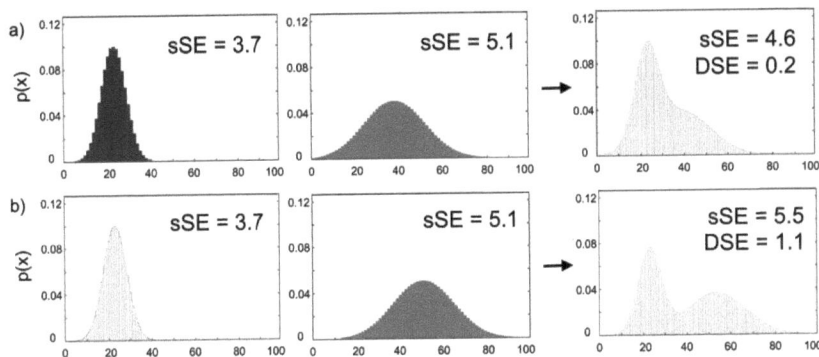

Fig. 2.6: SE and DSE calculations. Combinations of two data distributions are illustrated. (a) The data set in the center is more evenly distributed than the left one. Therefore, following the principles of Shannon entropy, the center distribution produces a higher sSE value. The combined sets result in the data distribution shown on the right side. The calculated DSE value is nearly zero because the single data sets show a similar distribution. (b) The data set in the center is shifted to the right. The combination of both data sets yields a higher DSE value, because the single distribution are more complementary to each other.

DSE values smaller than one, as typically produced by DSE calculations, should be emphasized. Finally, a ranking of decreasing molecular resemblance must be generated for a given set of compounds. Therefore we introduced the reciprocal Differential Shannon entropy defined as

$$rDSE = 1/|sDSE| \; ; \; \text{for sDSE} \neq 0 \qquad (2.4)$$

Here, sDSE is the scaled version of DSE calculated using sSE instead of SE values. The modified DSE metric allows ranking of compounds in decreasing order because small differences between data distributions (fragment populations) lead to high rDSE values, and vice versa.

Chapter 3

Assessment of Molecular Similarity

The majority of contemporary molecular similarity methods utilize structural or property descriptors for the generation of appropriate chemical reference spaces. The selection of descriptors most suitable for specific applications presents a difficult task [2] and might be influenced by subjective decisions. By contrast, randomly generated fragment populations do not depend on a predefined descriptor set or fragmentation scheme. The objective of this chapter is to demonstrate that fragment population can be successfully applied to detect molecular similarity relationships.

The analysis is divided into two steps. In Section 3.1 the potential of fragment populations to detect structural resemblance between single compounds is analyzed. Therefore, compounds with different biological activity are systematically fragmented with MolBlaster and ranked by means of the entropy-based rDSE similarity metric. The generated ranking lists are compared to a commonly used structure-based metric and deviations between the two rankings are recorded. These comparisons are used in Subsection 3.1.1 to determine the preferred fragmentation levels for diverse compound sets generating the most representative fragment populations. The evaluation of the rankings in Subsection 3.1.2 then provides evidence that structural resemblance can be assessed by focusing on chemical information provided by fragments. In Section 3.2 we go a step further and try to analyze if fragment populations might also encode specific structural information for a set of compounds with similar biological activity. Therefore, modifications of the MolBlaster approach are required that are introduced in Subsection 3.2.1. It is explained how a fragment profile for a given compound set is generated and how it can be used for similarity searching. In Subsection 3.2.2 the generated fragment profiles are applied to search databases for known active compounds. The obtained results are compared to reference calculations using standard methods, which demonstrates the ability of fragment profiles to detect structure-activity relationships.

3.1 Detection of Structural Resemblance

In order to evaluate the MolBlaster approach for molecular similarity detection, a reference system is needed to compare proposed relationships. Five pairs of molecules with similar activity were selected from the Molecular Drug Data Report (MDDR)[1]. The structures of these active compounds are shown in Figure 3.1. The molecules were binary encoded using MACCS keys [15], a fingerprint consisting of a set of 166 publicly available structural keys, and subjected to systematic pairwise comparisons using the Tanimoto coefficient (Tc) [59]. The Tanimoto coefficient calculates the structural similarity between a pair of compounds based on molecular fingerprint representations and is a standard similarity metric for chemoinformatics applications. It is defined as

$$\text{Tc}(A, B) = \frac{c}{a + b - c}$$

where a and b are the numbers of bits set on in the fingerprint of compounds A and B, and respectively c is the number of bits shared by both compounds. Thus, identical compounds yield a Tc value of 1.0, whereas completely distinct molecules produce a value of 0. Table 3.1 reports the resulting similarity ranking and confirms the presence of a spectrum of compound relationships with decreasing molecular similarity that span almost the entire Tc range. For MolBlaster calculations, MACCS-Tc similarity served as reference.

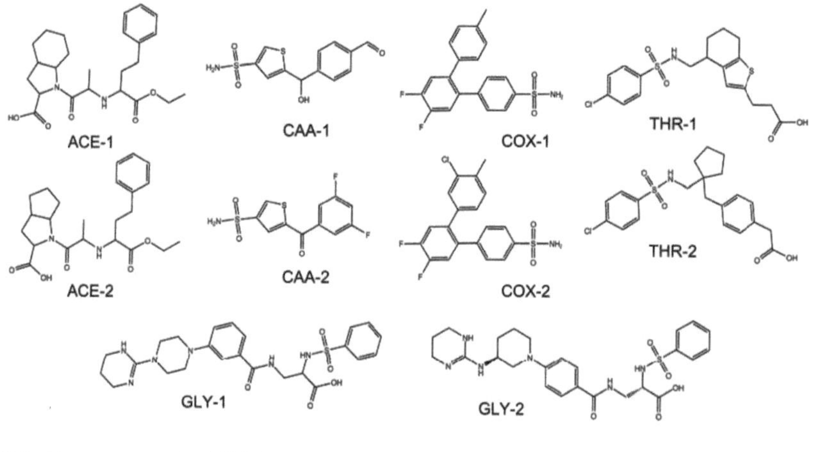

Fig. 3.1: **Test compounds.** MDDR activity class abbreviations: COX, cyclooxygenase-2 inhibitors; CAA, carbonic anhydrase inhibitors; GLY, glycoprotein IIb-IIIa inhibitors; ACE, acetylcholine esterase inhibitors; THR, thromboxane antagonists.

---
[1]Compound databases used throughout the thesis are described in Appendix A.

rank	molecule pair		Tc	
1	GLY-1	GLY-2	0.99	T 1
2	COX-1	COX-2	0.98	T 2
3	ACE-1	ACE-2	0.92	T 3
4	THR-1	THR-2	0.91	T 4
5	CAA-1	CAA-2	0.84	T 5
6	CAA-2	COX-1	0.79	T 6
7	CAA-2	COX-2	0.78	T 7
8	CAA-1	COX-1	0.65	T 8
9	CAA-1	COX-2	0.64	T 9
10	CAA-1	THR-1	0.64	T 10
11	CAA-2	THR-1	0.61	
12	GLY-1	THR-2	0.61	
13	GLY-2	THR-2	0.60	
14	GLY-1	THR-1	0.60	
15	GLY-2	THR-1	0.60	
16	CAA-1	THR-2	0.58	
17	COX-2	THR-2	0.55	
18	CAA-2	THR-2	0.55	
19	COX-2	THR-1	0.54	M 19
20	COX-1	THR-2	0.54	M 20
21	COX-1	THR-1	0.53	M 21
22	ACE-2	GLY-1	0.47	M 22
23	ACE-2	GLY-2	0.47	M 23
24	ACE-1	GLY-1	0.45	M 24
25	ACE-1	GLY-2	0.45	M 25
26	CAA-1	GLY-1	0.45	M 26
27	CAA-1	GLY-2	0.44	M 27
28	ACE-1	THR-1	0.41	M 28
29	ACE-2	THR-1	0.40	
30	COX-1	GLY-1	0.38	
31	CAA-2	GLY-1	0.38	
32	ACE-1	THR-2	0.38	
33	ACE-2	THR-2	0.38	
34	COX-2	GLY-1	0.38	
35	COX-1	GLY-2	0.38	
36	CAA-2	GLY-2	0.38	B 36
37	COX-2	GLY-2	0.38	B 37
38	ACE-1	CAA-1	0.27	B 38
39	ACE-2	CAA-1	0.27	B 39
40	ACE-1	CAA-2	0.20	B 40
41	ACE-2	CAA-2	0.20	B 41
42	ACE-1	COX-1	0.17	B 42
43	ACE-1	COX-2	0.16	B 43
44	ACE-2	COX-1	0.15	B 44
45	ACE-2	COX-2	0.15	B 45

Tab. 3.1: Tc-based similarity ranking of test molecule pairs. All possible pairwise comparisons were carried out for the molecules shown in Figure 3.1, and molecule pairs were ranked according to decreasing Tc values. "T", "M", and "B" designate the top 10 (most similar), midrange, and bottom (least similar) pairs, respectively. These 30 molecule pairs were labeled to permit an easy graphical comparison of this similarity ranking with the results of MolBlaster calculations.

3.1.1 Preferred Fragmentation Levels

To investigate which fragmentation levels were most suitable for similarity analysis, the number of deletions and iterations was systematically varied for pairwise comparison of the test compounds, and deviations from Tc ranking were calculated. Runs of varying length (with 100–5 000 iterations) were carried out permitting between five and 50 deletions per step. Compound pairs were ranked based on rDSE values, and deviations from the Tc ranking were calculated as the sum of deviations in rank positions over all compounds. Representative results are reported in Figure 3.2. Notable fluctuations in relative compound rankings were only observed during the initial ~2 000 iterations; then only minor differences could be detected. Thus, many copies of unique fragments were not required to reflect molecular similarity relationships.

By contrast, the fragmentation level had significant influence on the quality of similarity rankings. When permitting between 10 and 20 deletions per step, the correspondence between Tc- and fragment-based similarity rankings improved in nearly linear fashion; the smallest deviations occurred within the range of 27–29 deletions per step. Beyond 30 deletions, deviations from Tc rankings slightly increased again, probably because the fragments became on average too small. Figure 3.3 reports average fragment length as a function of the number of deletions. At preferred levels, the fragments contained on average six atoms (or four, when fragment frequency was considered). This appears to be an adequate trade-off between small fragments displaying little molecular structural information and large fragments that are too specific for their respective molecule. Thus, extensive but not exhaustive fragmentation is required for effective similarity detection.

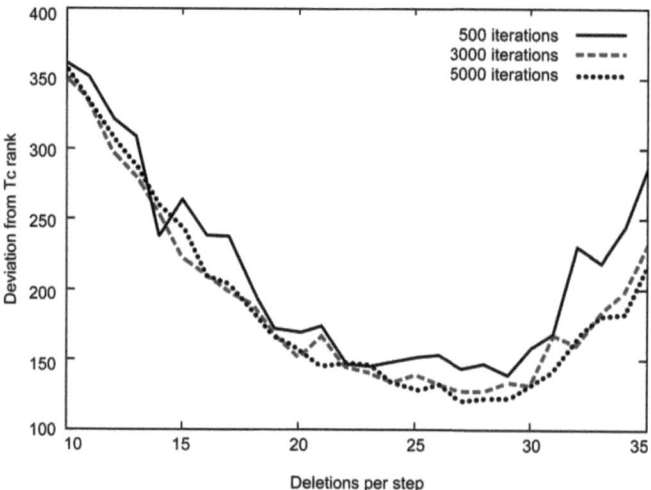

Fig. 3.2: Preferred fragmentation levels. Systematic variations of permitted deletions per step are shown for calculations of different length. In this example, rDSE values were used for fragment-based similarity ranking. The sum of deviations from MACCS Tc ranking were calculated as described in the text.

CHAPTER 3. SIMILARITY ASSESSMENT

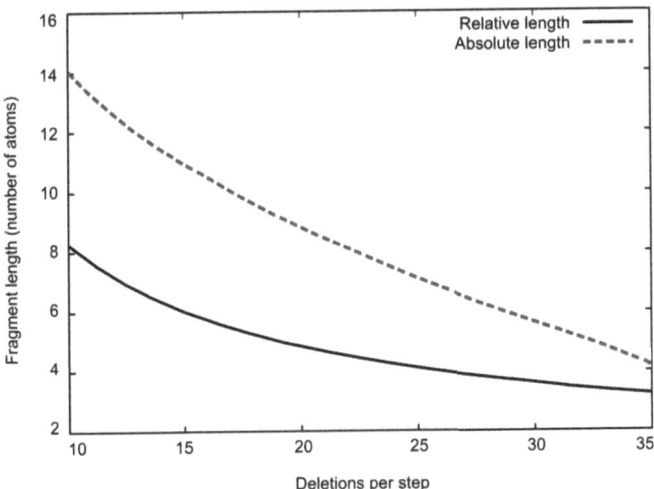

Fig. 3.3: Average fragment length. The average length of all fragments was calculated over all molecules as a function of the number of deletions. "Absolute length" reports the average size of distinct fragments, while "Relative length" takes the frequency of occurrence of the fragments into consideration. Calculations were carried out for 5 000 iterations.

3.1.2 Evaluation of Similarity Relationships

In order to verify the ability of the MolBlaster approach to detect molecular similarity relationships, the compound set was subjected to systematic fragmentation, and generated fragment populations were used to rank the compounds according to the entropy-based similarity metric rDSE. Afterwards the minimum deviation from a reference ranking was determined, which was observed in this case for 28 bond deletions per iteration step. In Table 3.2 the corresponding entropy-based similarity ranking is reported. The rDSE-based ranking closely reproduces the Tc-based ranking reported in Table 3.1 including the top, midrange, and bottom molecule pairs. For the top molecule pairs, covering a MACCS Tc range from 0.99 to 0.64, both rankings were nearly identical. Differences in single rank positions mostly occurred within the Tc range of 0.20 to 0.40 where many Tc values were similar or identical. Within this range, subtle differences in the fragment population led to improved discrimination between compounds compared to the Tc metric. Therefore, the rDSE was a more sensitive similarity metric, as it further distinguished between pairs of molecules having the same Tc value. Below a Tc-threshold of 0.20 the overlap of the fragment populations decreased rapidly, whereby distant similarity relationships between compounds were correctly detected.

In conclusion, the close correspondence between Tc- and rDSE-based compound pair rankings demonstrated that MolBlaster calculations could be successfully applied for the assessment of structural resemblance between compounds.

rank	molecule pair		rDSE	
1	GLY-1	GLY-2	212.55	T1
2	COX-1	COX-2	185.17	T2
3	ACE-1	ACE-2	160.23	T3
4	THR-1	THR-2	96.79	T4
5	COX-1	CAA-2	72.19	T6
6	COX-1	CAA-1	56.60	T8
7	CAA-2	CAA-1	51.26	T5
8	COX-2	CAA-2	50.52	T7
9	COX-2	CAA-1	41.13	T9
10	COX-2	THR-2	39.44	
11	COX-2	THR-1	36.77	M 19
12	CAA-1	THR-1	36.27	T 10
13	COX-1	THR-2	35.86	M 20
14	COX-1	THR-1	34.00	M 21
15	CAA-1	THR-2	33.51	
16	CAA-2	THR-1	29.81	
17	GLY-2	THR-2	28.45	
18	GLY-2	THR-1	27.99	
19	GLY-1	THR-1	26.66	
20	CAA-2	THR-2	26.52	
21	GLY-1	THR-2	26.50	
22	ACE-1	THR-2	25.30	
23	GLY-2	ACE-1	25.11	M 25
24	GLY-2	ACE-2	24.49	M 23
25	GLY-1	ACE-2	22.85	M 22
26	ACE-2	THR-2	22.82	
27	GLY-1	ACE-1	22.46	M 24
28	CAA-1	GLY-1	21.87	M 26
29	CAA-1	GLY-2	21.46	M 27
30	COX-1	GLY-1	21.21	
31	COX-1	GLY-2	21.20	
32	COX-2	GLY-1	20.93	
33	COX-2	GLY-2	20.88	B 37
34	CAA-2	GLY-1	20.54	
35	ACE-1	THR-1	20.43	M 28
36	CAA-2	GLY-2	20.35	B 36
37	ACE-2	THR-1	19.12	
38	COX-1	ACE-2	19.11	B 44
39	COX-1	ACE-1	17.88	B 42
40	COX-2	ACE-2	17.51	B 45
41	COX-2	ACE-1	16.75	B 43
42	CAA-1	ACE-2	16.46	B 39
43	CAA-1	ACE-1	15.78	B 38
44	CAA-2	ACE-2	14.67	B 41
45	CAA-2	ACE-1	14.42	B 40

Tab. 3.2: **rDSE-based similarity ranking of test molecule pairs.** The rDSE-based ranking was calculated for 28 possible deletions per step and 5 000 iterations. Molecular pairs are designated according to Table 3.1.

3.2 Detection of Structure-Activity Relationships

The results of this initial proof-of-principle study suggested the utility of fragment profiles in searching for active molecules within databases. For ligand-based virtual screening [60] and scaffold hopping [61], a similarity method must be capable of recognizing gradually decreasing similarity relationships including remote ones. However, before the MolBlaster approach could be applied for virtual screening, a number of challenges had to be met. First and foremost, the identification of structure-activity relationships goes beyond the mere detection of structural resemblance. Moreover, in database mining it is required to explore such relationships on a large scale and recognize the vast majority of database molecules as inactives. Therefore, fragment profile searching had to be sufficiently specific to correctly detect compounds having similar activity and discard others. Finally, sufficient computational efficiency is required in order to generate and process fragment profiles for many database molecules.

Evaluation of a Complexity-Independent MolBlaster Approach

A prerequisite for the application of the MolBlaster approach for virtual screening was to find an appropriate degree of fragmentation for diverse compound sets. The analysis of the preferred fragmentation level in Subsection 3.1.1 indicates that only a narrow range of possible bond deletions generates a fragment population sufficiently characteristic for test molecules. Thus, the optimal number of bond deletions may vary significantly for compounds belonging to structurally diverse classes. To establish a fragmentation scheme that ensured maximum information content of the fragment population irrespective of molecular topology, the number of bond deletions per iteration step was randomized for the MolBlaster approach. Seven randomly selected compound classes with varying degrees of heterogeneity, reported in Table 3.3, were subjected to pairwise comparisons in 20 fragmentation calculations. Because of the observations noted in Subsection 3.1.1, for each compound 3 000 MolBlaster iterations were carried out, which represented a reasonable compromise between accuracy and computation time. The compound pairs were ranked according to the rDSE metric and the resulting ranking list

code	biological activity	avg Tc
AA2	adrenergic ($\alpha 2$) agonists	0.38
ACE	ACE inhibitors	0.72
CHO	cholesterol esterase inhibitors	0.48
ESU	estrone sulfatase inhibitors	0.61
GLY	glycoprotein IIb-IIIa receptor-antagonists	0.59
LAC	lactamase (β) inhibitors	0.46
SQS	squalene synthetase inhibitors	0.50

Tab. 3.3: Compound activity classes. Compound set ACE is assembled from CMC, all other sets from the MDDR. To reflect the intra-class heterogeneity, for each set the average Tc (avg Tc) is reported, calculated from pairwise compound comparisons using MACCS structural keys.

	constant no. of deletions			random no. of deletions	
code	avg min dev	mean dev	opt del	avg dev	mean dev
AA2	84.2	0.68	16	85.5	0.60
ACE	23.0	0.59	13	26.9	0.24
CHO	46.1	0.28	21	44.5	0.29
ESU	83.6	0.75	10	85.4	0.77
GLY	91.9	0.81	29	99.4	0.91
LAC	61.2	0.26	26	67.2	0.63
SQS	129.2	0.68	32	140.1	1.32

Tab. 3.4: Comparison of different fragmentation methods. For fragmentation with constant numbers of bond deletions per iteration (constant no. of deletions), the average minimum deviation (avg min dev) in rank positions from a Tc-based pairwise compound ranking using MACCS structural keys is reported for five independent calculations varying the number of deletions. Also reported are the mean deviation (mean dev) and the number of bond deletions producing the minimum deviation (opt del). For the fragmentation process with randomized deletions per step and 20 independent trials, the average deviation in rank position (avg dev) and the mean deviation (mean dev) are given.

was compared to a Tc-based ranking using MACCS keys in order to quantify the deviations. These results were compared to equivalent calculations with varying number of constant deletions per step in order to find a preferred fragmentation level. The results obtained for all seven activity classes are summarized in Table 3.4. For each class, a different constant number of bond deletions produces lowest deviations from Tc ranking, ranging from 10 to 32 bonds, consistent with the topological diversity of the compound sets. Randomizing the number of permitted deletions gave results comparable to those obtained for optimized constant numbers. Only slightly higher deviations in six of seven cases were observed, although no class-directed optimization was carried out. A representative example for one activity class is shown in Figure 3.4. The number of permitted deletions per step was the major determinant of the average size of the resulting fragments. Randomization of deletions per step produced more diverse fragment populations than optimization, although observed differences were subtle. Because randomization essentially eliminated class-dependent differences in compound fragmentation, this procedure clearly is the method of choice for diverse compound classes where preferred fragmentation levels are not known a priori.

3.2.1 Methodology for Detection of Structure-Activity Relationships

Using the complexity-independent MolBlaster fragmentation scheme it was possible to generate unbiased fragment populations for compounds with distinct biological activity. So far, these individual populations have been used to detect structural resemblance between pairs of compounds. For the detection of structure-activity relationships only structural information provided by individual compounds could be considered. Therefore, it was attempted to generate a fragment profile for a set of compounds sharing similar biological activity.

CHAPTER 3. SIMILARITY ASSESSMENT

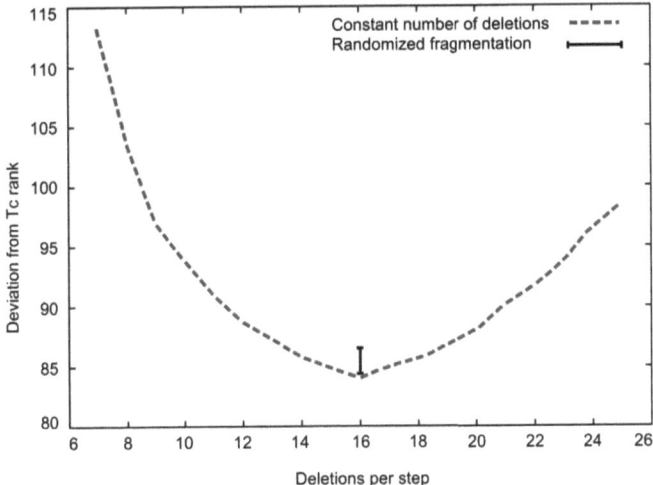

Fig. 3.4: Evaluation of fragmentation methods. For activity class AA2, the deviation of rDSE-based rank positions from a Tc-based ranking using MACCS structural keys are reported. The dashed line represents fragmentation using a constant number of deletions per step. The observed range of deviations for the randomized fragmentation scheme is represented by the black bar, positioned at the number of deletions producing the best results.

Generation of Compound-Class Specific Fragment Profiles

In Section 3.1 it was observed that compounds with similar biological activities showed higher overlap of their fragment populations than other compound pairs. This is explained by the *similarity property principle* [62], which states that structural similar molecules often show similar biological properties. Accordingly, a profile was derived from fragments that are shared by most active compounds and are therefore most characteristic of an activity class.

For a set of compounds having similar biological activity, individually generated fragment populations were merged into one set. Then, the frequency of occurrence of the fragments in the combined set was calculated. This process is illustrated in Figure 3.5. There is also illustrated that the frequencies of individual fragments were used to determine their information content for the activity class by means of Shannon entropy. If a fragment only occurs in one compound of the set, it is limited to one bin. Thus, following the principles of Shannon entropy analysis, the corresponding sSE value becomes zero. This indicates that the respective fragment contains no information about the activity class, but rather represents a single molecule. By contrast, if a fragment occurs with exactly the same frequency in all n test compounds, resulting in a maximum data dispersion and information content, the corresponding sSE value is one. Accordingly, this fragment has a high potential to characterize the activity class.

For the virtual screening calculations reported later in this chapter, fragments having a minimal sSE value of 0.75 are accepted to represent an activity class. This threshold was empirically determined on the basis of test calculations on diverse compound sets. Lowering the threshold value below 0.75 often led to a lower ranking of active compounds among top-scoring molecules, indicating that the additional fragments reduced the specificity of the profile for the activity class. With decreasing sSE value the fragments become increasingly specific for single active molecules, rather than for the set of compounds with similar activity. Therefore, the probability of a non-active compound to match a significant fraction of the expanded fragment profile increases, leading to a higher ranking of this compound.

Entropy-Based Scoring Metric

In the next step the potential of class-specific fragment profiles to detect structure-activity relationships within a large database was analyzed. Therefore, the overall similarity between a fragment profile of an activity class and the fragment population of a single database compound needed to be evaluated. Since for each fragment additional information about its class-specificity was determined, a new entropic scoring scheme was designed. This scoring function was termed *Proportional SE* (PSE) and defined as

$$\text{PSE} = \sum_i \frac{a}{b} \text{sSE}_{\text{AC}}(i) \qquad (3.1)$$

with $a = \min\{\text{Freq}_{\text{AC}}(i); \text{Freq}_{\text{DB}}(i)\}$ and $b = \max\{\text{Freq}_{\text{AC}}(i); \text{Freq}_{\text{DB}}(i)\}$. Here, $\text{Freq}_{\text{AC}}(i)$ is the class-specific frequency of fragment i in given activity class and $\text{Freq}_{\text{DB}}(i)$ the fragment frequency of a single database compound. The class-specific frequency of a fragment corresponds to the average frequency of occurrence in the compounds of the activity class. In other words, a (b) is the lower (higher) frequency of the fragment i in the profile of the activity class and the database compound, respectively. $\text{sSE}_{\text{AC}}(i)$ reports the sSE value for fragment i in the activity class, according to Figure 3.5.

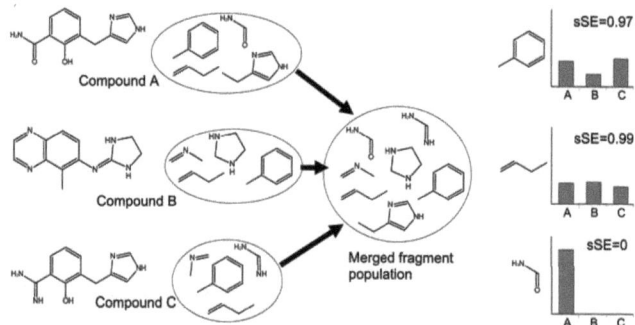

Fig. 3.5: Calculation of class specificity. The figure illustrates how sSE values are calculated to classify fragments on the basis of class specificity. First, the fragment populations of individual compounds of an activity class are combined into one set, while the frequency of occurrence of all fragments is recorded. Using these frequencies, histograms are generated, as shown on the right side. They monitor the distribution of fragments over all compounds. The information content of these distributions is then quantified using the sSE metric.

Weighting the sSE value by the frequency proportion favors the detection of database molecules that share many highly informative fragments with similar frequency. Such compounds produce a large cumulative PSE score as an indicator of molecular similarity. Applying this entropic formalism, virtual screening calculations generate a PSE-based ranking of database compounds relative to a class of known active compounds.

Dataset

For the virtual screening trials 15 different activity classes were used, reported in Table 3.5. Representative compounds from each class are shown in Figure 3.6. These compound sets were assembled from the Comprehensive Medicinal Chemistry (CMC) database, the Molecular Drug Data Report (MDDR), or taken from the literature [63]. In order to provide a spectrum of compound classes with medium to high structural diversity, classes were selected on the basis of intra-class average Tanimoto coefficient calculated using MACCS structural keys. The average Tc values for the 15 classes ranged from 0.38 to 0.72. For each class, about one-third of the compounds were randomly selected as reference molecules to determine common fragments and class-specific fragment frequencies; the remaining compounds were added to a source database as potential hits. To reduce chance effects, a certain number of random reference sets were selected for different series of calculations. Here, average results for 10 different reference sets are reported.

In order to analyze the predictive ability of fragment populations representing different levels of class-specific information content the fragment profiles of each activity class were grouped

code	biological activity	N	N_{ref}	avg Tc	dev
AA2	adrenergic ($\alpha 2$) agonists	35	12	0.38	0.15
ACE	ACE inhibitors	17	6	0.72	0.12
ANA	angiotensin II-AT antagonists	45	15	0.62	0.12
CAE	carbonic anhydrase II inhibitors	22	7	0.64	0.13
CAL	calpain inhibitors	28	9	0.48	0.14
CHO	cholesterol esterase inhibitors	30	10	0.48	0.18
DD1	dopamine (D1) agonists	30	10	0.54	0.15
ESU	estrone sulfatase inhibitors	35	12	0.61	0.11
GLY	glycoprotein IIb-IIIa receptor-antagonists	34	11	0.59	0.12
HIV	HIV protease inhibitors	18	6	0.67	0.14
KAP	κ agonists	25	8	0.55	0.15
KRA	kainic acid receptor antagonists	22	7	0.56	0.17
LAC	lactamase (β) inhibitors	29	10	0.46	0.18
LDL	upregulator of LDL receptor	30	10	0.49	0.22
SQS	squalene synthetase inhibitors	42	14	0.50	0.17

Tab. 3.5: Compound activity classes. Compound set ACE and CAE were assembled from CMC and all other sets from the MDDR, except HIV, which was taken from the literature. N gives the total number of compounds per class and N_{ref} the number of randomly selected reference compounds used to generate activity-class-specific fragment profiles and frequencies. The remaining active compounds were added to the source database as potential hits in virtual screening calculations. For each set, Tc similarity statistics from pairwise compound comparisons were calculated using MACCS structural keys, and average Tc (avg Tc) values as well as standard deviations (dev) are reported.

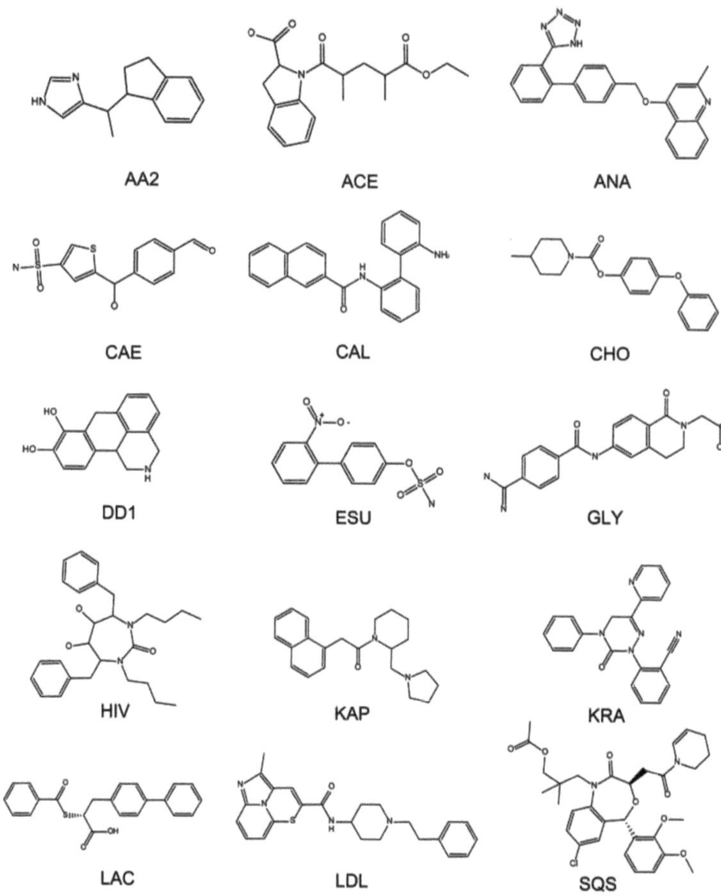

3.2. DETECTION OF STRUCTURE-ACTIVITY RELATIONSHIPS

Fig. 3.6: Representative compounds. For each of the activity classes studied here, a randomly selected molecule is shown.

into ranges of decreasing sSE values. Starting with fragments having an sSE value in the range [0.95–1.0], the lower boundary was further decreased in steps of 0.05 until the predefined threshold sSE value of 0.75 was reached. In Figure 3.7 an example of classified fragments from an activity class is shown.

3.2.2 Evaluation in Similarity Search Trials

The resulting fragment profiles were tested in virtual screening calculations, focusing on the question whether compounds having similar activity could be distinguished from very large numbers of database compounds on the basis of their fragmentation profiles. As a source database, a subset of 102 891 compounds with unique 2D molecular graphs was randomly

CHAPTER 3. SIMILARITY ASSESSMENT

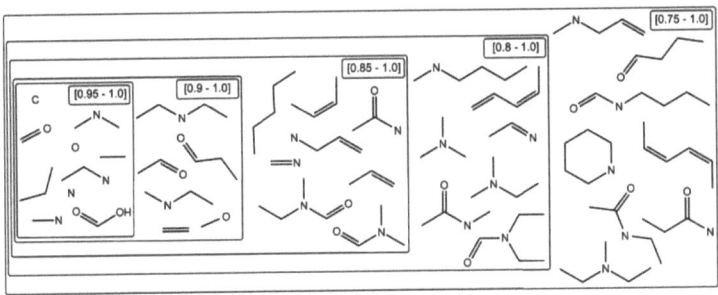

Fig. 3.7: Exemplary fragment classification into different sSE ranges. Shown are fragments with different sSE ranges taken from the fragment populations of GLY.

selected from the ZINC collection. Systematic screening trials were carried out using the PSE metric as scoring function and recovery rates for the top 100 or 1 000 compounds (i.e., for up to 1% of the source database) were recorded. Table 3.6 reports average results from 10 runs with varying reference sets for all activity classes for later discussion.

Compound recovery rates varied significantly among the activity classes and were also much influenced by the choice of different sSE ranges and thus fragmentation levels. Overall, the obtained results were promising. For seven classes, recovery rates of >50–100% were obtained for only 100 selected database compounds, and for the remaining classes, the corresponding recovery rates at preferred fragmentation levels ranged from ~25% to 48%. Selecting of 1% of the database compounds, nine classes displayed recovery rates of >75–100%. These findings demonstrate that molecular fragment profiles can be successfully used as queries for database searching and that significant recovery rates are already achieved for small compound selection sets. This can be seen in Table 3.6, which shows that recovery rates did not dramatically increase when selecting 10 times more database compounds. This suggests that large-scale fragment profile comparisons have a significant degree of specificity. The results also illustrate that structurally homogeneous classes such as ACE produced the best compound recovery rates, as one would expect. However, even for distinctly diverse classes such as AA2, recovery rates of ~20% were achieved within the 100 top-scoring database compounds. These findings indicate that fragment profile searching can explore diverse structure-activity relationships and that it has significant scaffold-hopping potential [61]. This point is further supported by the inspection of recovered compounds and reference molecules used to detect them. Representative results in Figure 3.8 show that reference compounds and correctly identified hits frequently had different core structures.

Computational Benchmarking

Benchmark calculations revealed that 1 000 MolBlaster iterations required between 0.8 and 1.4 seconds per molecule on a 3.6 GHz processor. During the virtual screening trials, 30–110 database molecules were processed per second of CPU time, depending on the size of

3.2. DETECTION OF STRUCTURE-ACTIVITY RELATIONSHIPS

sSE range	RR_{100}	RR_{1K}	RR_{100}	RR_{1K}	RR_{100}	RR_{1K}
	AA2		ACE		ANA	
[0.95–1.0]	4.8	19.1	90.0	92.7	80.3	93.0
[0.90–1.0]	10.0	23.9	88.2	95.5	85.3	94.3
[0.85–1.0]	17.8	30.9	91.8	100	87.0	94.3
[0.80–1.0]	20.0	35.2	94.5	100	92.0	94.3
[0.75–1.0]	27.8	37.4	95.5	100	93.0	94.7
	CAE		CAL		CHO	
[0.95–1.0]	62.7	79.3	11.1	24.2	10.5	20.0
[0.90–1.0]	58.0	78.0	23.2	48.4	29.0	40.5
[0.85–1.0]	57.3	76.0	28.4	55.3	34.5	47.0
[0.80–1.0]	55.4	75.3	34.2	53.7	47.0	58.0
[0.75–1.0]	53.3	73.3	40.5	56.9	47.0	57.0
	DD1		ESU		GLY	
[0.95–1.0]	0	7.9	48.3	61.7	62.6	86.6
[0.90–1.0]	25.8	63.2	78.7	82.2	46.5	74.4
[0.85–1.0]	32.6	70.5	85.7	88.3	47.0	69.6
[0.80–1.0]	50.0	76.8	85.7	89.6	39.1	60.0
[0.75–1.0]	56.3	78.4	85.7	91.3	40.0	62.2
	HIV		KAP		KRA	
[0.95–1.0]	98.3	100	17.7	32.9	11.3	33.3
[0.90–1.0]	100	100	28.8	51.8	16.7	32.7
[0.85–1.0]	99.2	100	35.9	58.8	19.3	32.7
[0.80–1.0]	98.3	100	37.1	60.0	18.7	36.6
[0.75–1.0]	98.3	100	38.3	65.0	17.3	27.4
	LAC		LDL		SQS	
[0.95–1.0]	17.9	46.8	2.5	8.5	25.7	56.8
[0.90–1.0]	16.3	43.7	5.5	23.0	31.8	49.3
[0.85–1.0]	21.6	48.7	18.0	30.0	35.7	52.2
[0.80–1.0]	21.6	45.3	29.5	41.5	36.1	52.5
[0.75–1.0]	24.7	43.7	39.0	46.0	35.4	52.9

Tab. 3.6: Virtual screening trials Average recovery rates (RR; in percent) are reported for the top-scoring 100 (RR_{100}), and 1 000 (RR_{1K}) compounds for each activity class and different sSE ranges of the fragment populations.

the involved fragment populations, thus permitting the screening of large compound sets in a reasonable time.

Analysis of Fragment Profiles

After confirming that fragment profile methods were capable of consistently detecting active compounds in database search calculations and assessing its search capacity, the influence of profile size on compound recovery was analyzed. In the majority of cases, extension of the fragment-qualifying sSE range increased compound recovery rates. This indicated that larger fragment populations had higher information content, leading to similarity analysis at higher resolution and increasingly accurate compound ranking. Preferred sSE ranges for fragment selection substantially varied among the different activity classes. For 8 of 15 classes, the [0.75–1.0] range gave the best results. For the other classes, more narrowly defined sSE ranges were preferred, reflecting class-specific differences in fragment profiling. For example, for CAE

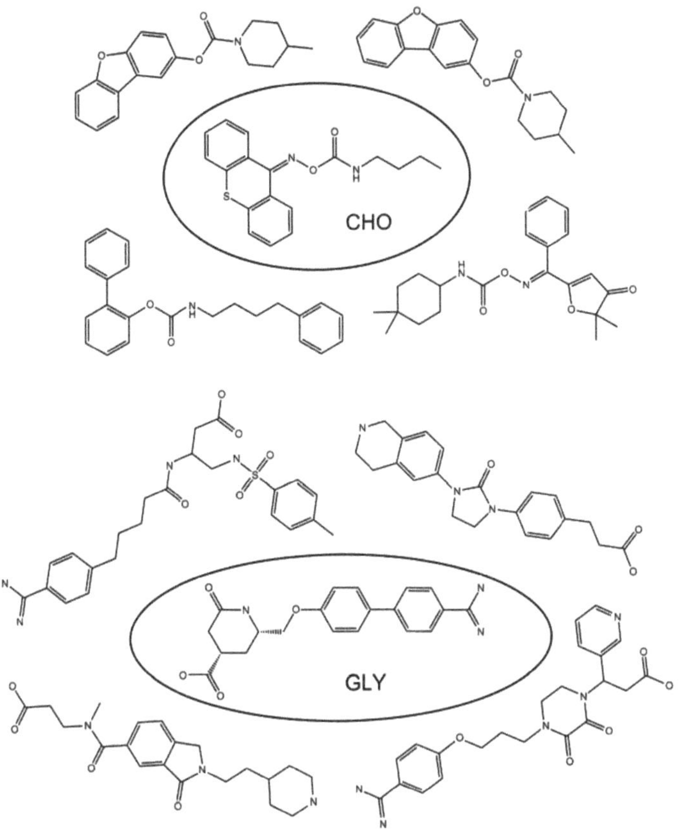

Fig. 3.8: Retrieval of active compounds. Shown are examples of correctly identified hits among the top-scoring 100 database compounds for activity classes CHO (top) and GLY (bottom). Active reference molecules are encircled.

and GLY, the smallest sSE range gave the best results. In other cases, such for ESU or SQS, intermediate levels performed best. However, with only one exception (GLY) among the seven classes that produced best recovery rates at small or medium size sSE ranges, the results were similar to those obtained for the [0.75–1.0] range. Therefore, for virtual screening trials the sSE range [0.75–1.0] should present a reasonable choice for targeting many different activity classes in fragment profile searching.

Furthermore, differences in search performance between single trials for an activity class could be attributed to differences in fragment populations derived from distinct reference sets. This can be observed in Table 3.7 that summarizes the recovery rates obtained for 10 unique reference sets selected for activity class ESU. Recovery rates were very similar in 6 of 10 cases but significantly lower in four others. Thus, although many reference sets produced comparable recovery rates, differences as a consequence of reference set composition could also be observed.

ref set	avg Tc	RR_{100}	RR_{500}	RR_{1K}
1	0.61	69.7	87.0	91.3
2	0.60	4.3	21.7	21.7
3	0.59	0.0	4.3	13.0
4	0.64	13.0	26.1	34.8
5	0.65	78.3	82.6	82.6
6	0.65	78.3	82.6	82.6
7	0.64	78.3	82.6	82.6
8	0.60	73.9	82.6	82.6
9	0.61	8.7	30.4	43.5
10	0.65	78.3	82.6	82.6

Tab. 3.7: Recovery rates for individual reference sets. For activity class ESU, average recovery rates (RR; in percent) for 10 randomly selected unique reference sets are reported within sSE range [0.95–1.0]. Average MACCS Tc values (avg Tc) are reported for a pairwise comparison of reference compounds.

An extreme example is provided by the comparison of reference set 3 with one of the best performing sets, e.g. set 5. Here, one of the randomly generated reference sets produced recovery rates of ~80% already for 100 selected compounds, whereas the other essentially failed to recover active compounds. Detailed examination revealed that the fragment population derived from the well-performing set was nearly three times larger than the other. Taken together, these findings indicate that differences in fragment numbers and distributions are important for accurate compound ranking.

Reference Calculations

To compare the performance of fragment profile searching with that of standard methods, reference calculations with four different types of 2D fingerprints with varying complexity were carried out. Namely MACCS keys, MPMFP, Molprint 2D and the Daylight fingerprint were used. As a purely structural fragment-based design MACCS keys were selected (166 keys). MPMFP [64] is a hybrid fingerprint consisting of 171 keys that combines structural features and binary transformed molecular property descriptors. Molprint 2D [26] derives keys from the connectivity tables of a molecule and combines varying numbers of strings that represent unique atom environments organized in distance layers. Finally, the Daylight fingerprint captures connectivity pathways in molecules and is often considered a gold standard in the field, because it pioneered the development of hashed 2D fingerprints. Here a version consisting of 2 048 bits was calculated using the Daylight toolkit.

Although fingerprinting is conceptually distinct from fragment profiling, fingerprint searches were chosen as reference calculations because they also produce a similarity-based ranking of database compounds. Thus, the number of active molecules occurring within a specific number of top-scoring database compounds can be easily compared. As a multiple template-based search strategy, the centroid approach [65] was applied, because fragment profiles searches also make use of information from multiple reference compounds. Following this strategy,

CHAPTER 3. SIMILARITY ASSESSMENT

an average fingerprint vector is calculated from the individual fingerprints of all available reference compounds and compared to database molecules using the general formulation of the Tanimoto coefficient for floating-point values [59], rather than for binary representations. The recovery rates for the reference calculations are reported in Table 3.8. They are compared to the results obtained in the fragment screening trials for the top-scoring 100 database compounds. Observed differences in search performance were overall comparable in a number of cases. For example, for seven activity classes, differences between all four fingerprints and the fragment profiling method were within ~15%. Overall, Molprint 2D performed best in these calculations, followed by MPMFP, fragment profiling, Daylight, and MACCS structural keys. Of the fingerprints used here for comparison, Molprint 2D represents by far the highest level of complexity. However, differences in search performance between these fingerprints were often subtle. For example, for 10 of 15 classes, differences between Molprint 2D and Daylight were within ~15%. Thus, the 2D fingerprints used here frequently produced comparable search results, despite significant differences in their design and complexity. Random fragment profiling gave better results than defined MACCS structural keys in 11 of 15 cases, although differences in recovery rates were here also within ~15% for 13 activity classes. Thus, taken together, fragment profile searching performed at least comparably well to widely used 2D similarity search tools, without the need to use conventional or high-complexity descriptors.

class	frag profile	MACCS	MPMFP	Daylight	Molprint 2D
AA2	27.8	20.9	30.9	28.3	33.9
ACE	95.5	81.1	95.5	80.9	100.0
ANA	93.0	65.7	79.4	91.7	85.0
CAE	62.7	56.7	82.0	37.8	52.0
CAL	40.5	26.8	38.4	22.6	53.7
CHO	47.0	49.0	50.0	58.0	60.5
DD1	56.3	61.5	72.0	26.0	59.0
ESU	85.7	79.6	80.0	65.2	95.2
GLY	62.6	48.3	65.7	16.5	51.7
HIV	100	70.0	82.5	93.3	74.3
KAP	38.3	25.9	38.8	24.7	31.8
KRA	19.3	22.7	38.7	51.3	63.3
LAC	24.7	35.8	37.7	51.1	36.0
LDL	39.0	28.0	46.5	43.5	52.0
SQS	36.1	34.3	42.9	40.7	44.6

Tab. 3.8: Reference calculations. Reported are the best recovery rates (in percent) for the top-scoring 100 compounds using fragment profiling (frag profile) in combination with our PSE similarity metric and four different fingerprints. For similarity searching using these fingerprints, the centroid approach was applied and Tc values were calculated for compound ranking.

3.3 Summary and Conclusions

In this chapter it is shown that randomly generated fragment populations encode sufficient chemical information of source molecules to mirror molecular similarity relationships between them. For the analysis and comparison of molecular fragment profiles, entropy-based measures adapted from information theory provide a sensitive similarity metric. Fragment populations display maximum information content for an average fragment size of approximately six atoms, which requires extensive fragmentation of the test molecules. This can be achieved by selecting a constant number of bond deletions that depends on the size and topological complexity of the compounds. After a threshold of 2 000 fragmentation steps, the diversity of fragment population converges. Randomizing the number of bond deletions also generates informative fragment populations. This approach offers the advantage of being independent of the complexity of the compounds and is therefore generally preferred.

In virtual screening trials, fragment profiles display significant specificity and produce promising recovery rates for diverse active compounds. Correctly identified hits are among high-scoring compounds and are often structurally distinct from reference compounds, thus indicating the potential of fragment profile searching for scaffold hopping. In reference calculations fragment profiles show performance comparable to established 2D similarity search tools of higher complexity.

Chapter 4

Mining of Activity-Class Derived Fragment Profiles

Taken together, the findings in the previous chapter suggested that random molecular fragment populations must contain specific information about characteristic compound features. This raised a number of questions. What is this information? How can class-specific elements be identified? What can one learn about class specific features from information contained in random fragment populations?

Motivated by these questions, in Section 4.1 fragment profiles are carefully analyzed, providing evidence that subsets of class-characteristic fragments mostly account for the predictive ability of profiles. To identify such signature fragments, a method is designed in Section 4.2 that systematically explores the dependency of fragment occurrence among compounds with similar biological activity. Mining of these dependency relationships between fragments reveals the existence of Activity-Class Characteristic Substructures (ACCS). In Section 4.3 the information content of ACCS is evaluated in virtual screening trials on structurally diverse datasets. Finally, the results of these search calculations are compared to other commonly used fingerprint representations.

4.1 Mining of Randomly Generated Fragment Profiles

In order to explore the relationships between class-specific features of fragment profiles and their ability to detect active compounds, the composition of fragment profiles was analyzed in detail.

4.1.1 Composition of Fragment Profiles

In the light of the findings reported in the previous chapter, the sSE range-dependence of fragment distributions was further analyzed. For clarity, results obtained for four representative activity classes (see Table 4.1) are reported here. The results for the remaining 11

4.1. MINING OF RANDOM FRAGMENT PROFILES

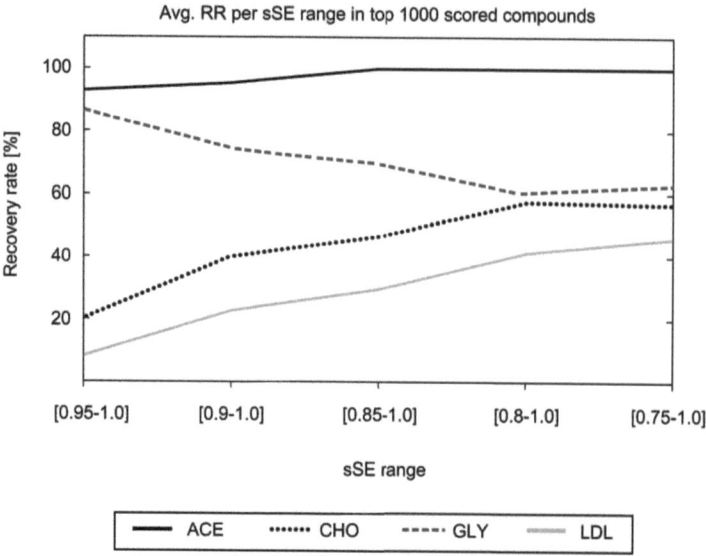

Fig. 4.1: Results of virtual screening trials. The figure reports average recovery rates for different sSE ranges and the top-scoring 1 000 compounds.

compound sets are provided in Appendix B and confirm major findings. As a reference, the recovery rates for these four classes in the virtual screening trials are reported in Figure 4.1. The average number of fragments for each sSE range is given in Table 4.2. The specificity of fragment profiles for activity classes was analyzed by calculating the percentage of fragments that frequently occurred in the database, i.e. in at least 10 000 ZINC compounds (~10% of the database). Such fragments provide a nonspecific fragmentation background during search calculations.

Table 4.2 shows that the number of fragments consistently increased when the sSE range was expanded, as one would expect. However, the number of fragments for each sSE range significantly differed between classes. For example, in the sSE range [0.95–1.0], 72 fragments were found for ACE, whereas for LDL only six were found. Furthermore generated fragments

code	biological activity	N	N_{baits}	avg Tc	dev
ACE	ACE inhibitors	17	6	0.72	0.12
CHO	cholesterol esterase inhibitors	30	10	0.48	0.18
GLY	glycoprotein IIb-IIIa receptor-antagonists	34	11	0.59	0.12
LAC	lactamase (β) inhibitors	29	10	0.46	0.18

Tab. 4.1: Compound activity classes. Subset of the activity classes used in virtual screening trials (see Table 3.5 on page 29). N gives the total number of compounds per class and N_{baits} the number of randomly selected bait compounds. To get insights to the diversity of each class, the average Tc (avg Tc) and its standard deviation (dev) is calculated.

CHAPTER 4. MINING FRAGMENT PROFILES

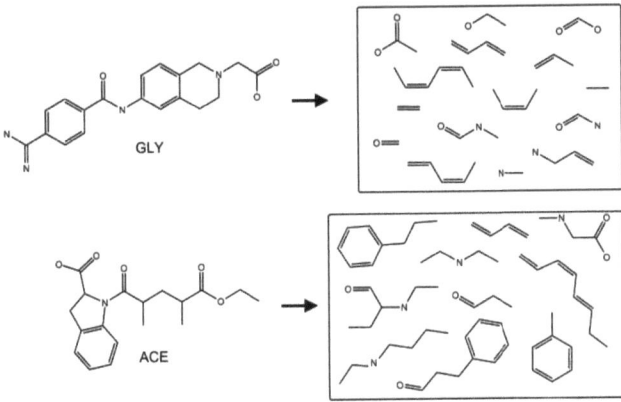

Fig. 4.2: Representative fragment populations. For GLY (top) and ACE (bottom) fragments having a sSE value within the range [0.95–1.0] are illustrated. The molecules on the left are representatives for their activity classes.

also varied in size, as illustrated in Figure 4.2. Variations in fragment number and their average size were largely due to relative differences in intra-class structural diversity. There was a correlation between the average Tc value of an activity class and the number and size of their fragments: compounds in structurally homogeneous classes had the tendency to produce more and larger common fragments than increasingly diverse classes. Importantly, Table 4.2 shows that each activity class had a significant number of fragments that did not occur in the fragmentation background. In general, increasing the number of activity-class unique fragments resulted in a higher number of detected

sSE range	avg no. frgmts	% freq set	avg no. frgmts	% freq set
	ACE		CHO	
[0.95–1.0]	71.5	61.2	7.5	97.0
[0.90–1.0]	114.2	48.7	20.3	91.2
[0.85–1.0]	154.6	41.7	38.1	78.6
[0.80–1.0]	181.2	37.0	65.9	67.1
[0.75–1.0]	218.7	32.5	94.9	55.8
	GLY		LDL	
[0.95–1.0]	16.2	99.4	5.7	98.5
[0.90–1.0]	28.3	94.2	13.1	92.9
[0.85–1.0]	42.8	86.3	27.9	85.6
[0.80–1.0]	62.0	73.8	45.1	77.0
[0.75–1.0]	86.9	61.1	74.3	66.3

Tab. 4.2: Size and Composition of Fragment Sets. For each activity class, the average number of fragments (avg no. frgmts) for specified sSE ranges is reported as well as the percentage of those fragments also contained in the set of most frequently occurring fragments (% freq set). This set consists of all fragments that are also produced by at least 10 000 ZINC database compounds.

known active compounds. This was observed in 13 of 15 cases. However, the performance of the fragment profiles during virtual screening trials could not be rationalized only by the number of activity-class unique fragments. For example, the compound set GLY showed best recovery rates for sSE range [0.95–1.0], where only 0.6% of the fragments are unique to the activity class. Similarly, for class CHO (and others), the preferred sSE range was narrower than [0.75–1.0]. Therefore, no clear correlation could be determined between the increase of activity-class unique fragments and the increase in recovery.

These findings suggested that a limited number of *signature* fragments might have the same information content as a larger set of perhaps more redundant fragments. Therefore, it was attempted to generate a hierarchical organization of fragments according to their ability to characterize individual compound sets. The study of such fragment hierarchies was thought to reveal why small sets of class-unique fragments had predictive utility comparable to larger fragment sets.

4.2 Detection of Fragment Dependency Hierarchies

To explore the relationships between substructures in a fragment population at the molecular level of detail a novel method is introduced [66]. It is designed to determine systematically whether there are dependencies of fragment co-occurrences. Therefore, it is attempted to identify and quantify fragment dependencies and organize fragment populations according to their dependence relationships. The conceptual framework developed here is annotated according to an illustrative example.

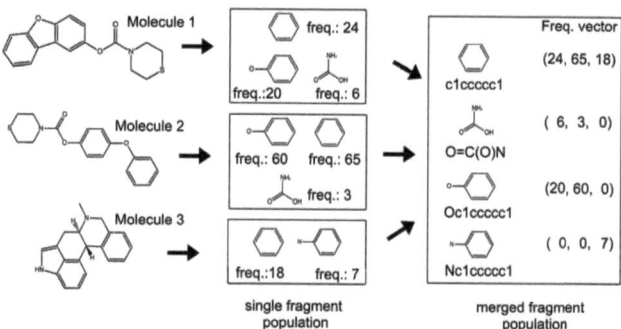

Fig. 4.3: Generation of fragment profiles. An ordered set of molecules is subjected to random fragmentation. After generation of individual fragment populations the frequency of occurrence is determined for each fragment. When individual fragment populations are combined, frequency vectors are generated that record the relative frequency of occurrence in all molecules. Molecule 1 and 2 are cholesterol esterase inhibitors, while molecule 3 is a dopamine D1 antagonist.

CHAPTER 4. MINING FRAGMENT PROFILES

4.2.1 Methodology for Mining Dependency Relationships

Let MS = {Molecule$_1$, Molecule$_2$, ..., Molecule$_N$} be an ordered set of N arbitrarily assembled molecules and FragPop(MS) the merged fragment set derived from single fragment populations. Each fragment *frag* is associated with a frequency vector fv, where the i-th item is defined as

$$\text{fv}(frag)(i) = \text{freq}(frag, i)$$

i.e. the frequency of the fragment in the population of the i-th molecule from MS. The generation of frequency vectors is illustrated in Figure 4.3. The vectors are used to project fragments into an N-dimensional reference system constituted by MS. Each axis of this coordinate system represents the frequency of occurrence of a fragment in a specific molecule during the fragmentation process. In Figure 4.4 the coordinate system for the molecules in Figure 4.3 is shown. This conceptual framework makes it possible to define dependency relationships between pairs of fragments. In principle, the occurrence of a fragment *frag$_{dep}$* within an activity class can only depend on another fragment *frag$_{cond}$*, if *frag$_{dep}$* is generated in the subset of molecules, from which *frag$_{cond}$* is derived. Furthermore, the frequency of *frag$_{dep}$* is not allowed to exceed the frequency of *frag$_{cond}$* for all molecules. These conditions can be formulated as follows:

$$\forall\, 1 \leq i \leq N : \text{fv}(frag_{dep})(i) \leq \text{fv}(frag_{cond})(i) \tag{4.1}$$

where $\forall$ is a mathematical quantifier that means "for all". In the case that two fragments have been produced for all molecules with equal frequencies, no dependency relationship can be established. Thus, a dependent fragment *frag$_{dep}$* has to be produced by at least one molecule with a lower frequency than *frag$_{cond}$*:

$$\exists\, 1 \leq i \leq N : \text{fv}(frag_{dep})(i) < \text{fv}(frag_{cond})(i) \tag{4.2}$$

Here, the quantifier $\exists$ means "there exists".

In order to quantify the degree of dependency between fragments, a new function *dep* is introduced:

$$\text{dep}(frag_{dep}, frag_{cond}) = \delta \sum_{i=1}^{N} \text{fv}(frag_{dep})(i)/\text{fv}(frag_{cond})(i) \tag{4.3}$$

where the delta operator is defined as:

$$\delta = \begin{cases} 1 & \text{if} \quad \forall\, 1 \leq i \leq N : \text{fv}(frag_{dep})(i) \leq \text{fv}(frag_{cond})(i) \\ & \text{and} \quad \exists\, 1 \leq i \leq N : \text{fv}(frag_{dep})(i) < \text{fv}(frag_{cond})(i), \\ 0 & \text{else} \end{cases}$$

and combines the dependency condition stated in 4.1 and 4.2. If one of both conditions is violated, the delta operator (and thus the function) returns the value zero. Non-zero dependency values indicate a conditional probability relationship between two fragments. For a conditional fragment, the fragment with the largest dependency value is most closely related to and de-

4.2. DETECTION OF FRAGMENT HIERARCHIES

dependent fragments	conditional fragments			
	c1ccccc1	O=C(O)N	Oc1ccccc1	Nc1ccccc1
c1ccccc1	-	0	0	0
O=C(O)N	0.30	-	**0.35**	0
Oc1ccccc1	**1.75**	0	-	0
Nc1ccccc1	**0.39**	0	0	-

Tab. 4.3: Quantification of fragment dependency. For the fragments shown in Figure 4.3, dependency values are calculated for all possible fragment pair combinations. Maximum values for dependent fragments are written in bold.

pendent on it. Table 4.3 reports the calculated dependency values for the example fragments shown in Figure 4.3. For all fragments, it is possible to determine a set of conditional fragments $CF(frag)$ yielding the largest dependency value for dependent fragments. This set is defined as:

$$CF(frag_i) = \{frag_k \in \text{FragPop} | \neg \exists frag_j : \text{dep}(frag_i, frag_j) > \text{dep}(frag_i, frag_k)\}$$

where $\neg \exists$ means "there exists no". For individual fragments, this set can be empty. Such fragments are fundamental in the profile because their occurrence does not depend on any other fragments.

In Figure 4.4 so derived maximal fragment dependency relationships are shown. For fragment populations derived from any set of molecules, a corresponding graph structure can be built after calculating dependency values. In order to determine essential fragment pathways leading to individual molecules, fragment populations were complemented with SMILES representations of all source molecules. These "meta"-fragments are assigned a frequency vector where the dimension representing each individual molecule is set to one, whereas all other values are set to zero (e.g. the second molecule of the three-member compound set has the frequency vector

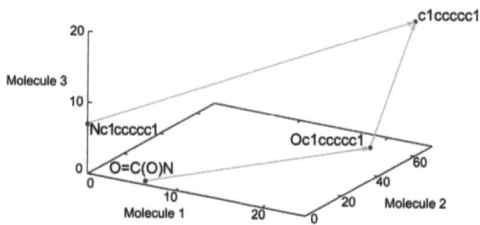

Fig. 4.4: Mapping of fragments to a molecular coordinate systems. For the molecule set in Figure 4.3, a reference system is established where fragments (encoded as SMILES) are positioned based on their frequency vectors. Dots indicate fragment positions, arrows represent maximum dependency relationships between fragments.

(0, 1, 0)). This procedure guarantees that intact molecules are always positioned at the termini of a fragment hierarchy. Furthermore, it simplifies the tree representation because pathways that do not terminate at individual molecules can be eliminated, as such fragment paths cannot have signature character.

Interpretation of Fragment Dependency

A prototypic tree representation of the relationships in Figure 4.4 is depicted in Figure 4.5. On the basis of this graph, the meaning of fragment dependency relationships can be rationalized. The three molecules shown in Figure 4.3 produce a pathway leading from benzene (SMILES string c1ccccc1) to the phenol ring (Oc1ccccc1) and the carbamic acid (O=C(O)N) in the left branch of the graph, whereas the right branch leads to aniline (Nc1ccccc1).

The frequency vector shows that benzene was produced by all three molecules. However, only a subset of these molecules produced the phenol ring and carbamic acid. The dependency relationship means that whenever the phenol ring was generated, the fragment profile also contained benzene. Furthermore, whenever carbamic acid was produced, the fragment profile also contained the phenol ring. This means that the occurrence of the phenol ring in the fragment profile is dependent on the presence of benzene that was generated more frequently within this subset of molecules. Similarly, the occurrence of carbamic acid is dependent on the presence of the phenol ring. By contrast, aniline was produced for a different molecule subset than the phenol ring or carbamic acid. Therefore, no dependency exists between these substructures.

Importantly, pathways like the left branch in Figure 4.5 can only exist for subsets of test molecules, as indicated by the corresponding frequency vectors of the fragments. Therefore, the simultaneous presence of the three fragments discussed above becomes a signature for two of the three test molecules shown in Figure 4.3. Additionally, in this example we can assign a biological activity to the phenol ring and the carbamic acid because these fragments were only found in cholesterol esterase inhibitors. Such fragments that are generated only by molecules of a certain compound class are termed *Activity Class Characteristic Substructures* (ACCS). In the following, ACCS are defined as fragments that occur in at least two molecules belonging to the same activity class but none of the as background declared database compounds.

It should be mentioned that fragment dependencies are not necessarily substructure relationships. For example, there is a frequency-based dependency relationship between benzene and the carbamic acid in Figure 4.5, but no structural relationship because the smaller fragment is not a substructure of benzene. Thus, the fragment relationships analyzed herein go beyond the assessment of structural resemblance and capture the conditional probability of fragment occurrence.

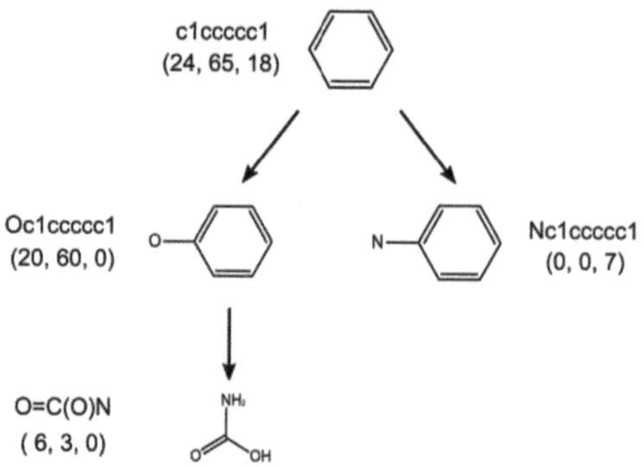

4.2. DETECTION OF FRAGMENT HIERARCHIES

```
                c1ccccc1
               (24, 65, 18)


Oc1ccccc1                      Nc1ccccc1
(20, 60, 0)                    (0, 0, 7)


O=C(O)N
( 6, 3, 0)
```

Fig. 4.5: Dependency graph. Shown is a graph representation capturing the fragment dependencies in Figure 4.4, as described in the text.

4.2.2 Analysis of Fragment Dependency Hierarchies

In order to mine random fragment populations and establish fragment dependencies, test sets consisting of different known active and background database compounds were assembled and subjected to MolBlaster fragmentation. For these combined sets, a fragment profile was generated and dependency values were systematically calculated using the *dep* function. On the basis of these dependency values, fragment populations were organized in graphs, that were further annotated with activity information.

Dataset

The exemplary test set consisted of 15 compounds, two times five belonging to two different activity classes of the MDDR and five randomly taken from ZINC. The active compounds were neurokinin NK2 receptor antagonists (NK2) and thromboxane antagonists (THR). The structures of the complete test set are shown in Figure 4.6. For illustrative purposes the size of this molecule set was limited because graphs for representing fragment dependencies quickly become very large and complex, which hinders intuitive visual analysis. Calculations on larger molecule sets and more than three classes per set were also carried out. Comparison revealed that the basic findings reported here did not depend on the size of the test sets, but rather on their intrinsic structural diversity.

For comparison of active compounds, Tanimoto similarity was calculated using the MACCS fingerprint. Potential activities of the ZINC compounds are unknown, and they were thus considered decoys in the analysis. All test molecules were fragmented over 3 000 MolBlaster iterations, and tree graphs were drawn with Graphviz.

Random fragment profiles and dependency graphs can be calculated for arbitrary sets of molecules, but the presence of known active compounds makes it possible to annotate the fragment pathways with activity data. In order to further simplify the evaluation of depen-

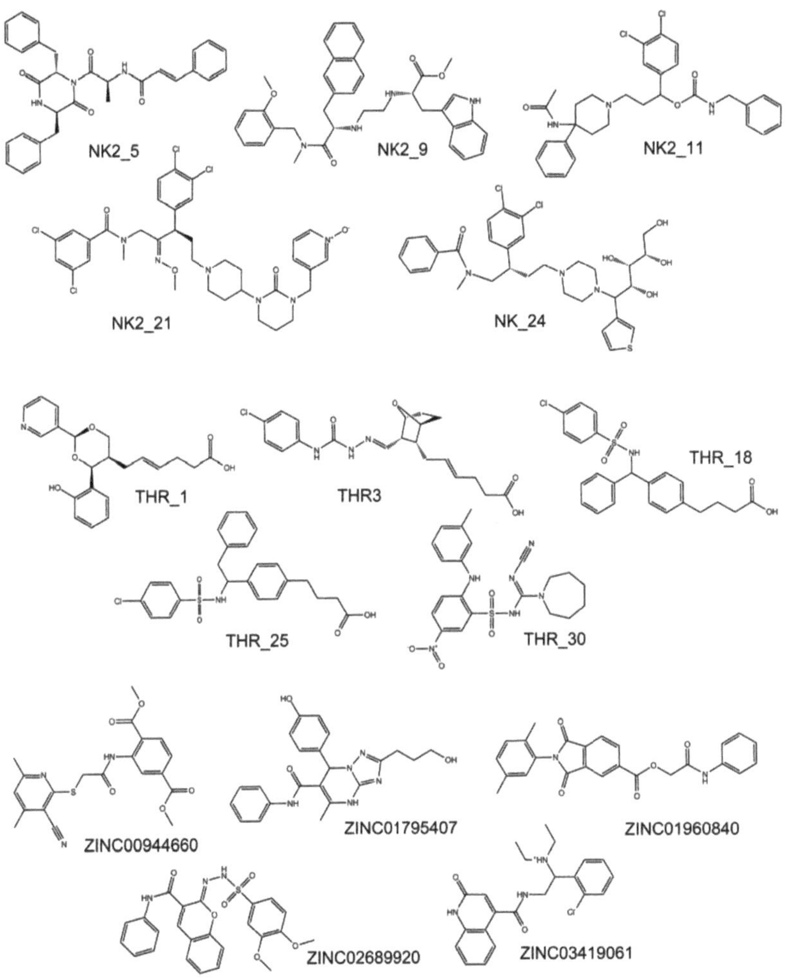

Fig. 4.6: Molecular test set. Structures of neurokinin NK2 receptors antagonists (NK2), thromboxane antagonists (THR) and ZINC molecules are shown, for which random fragment populations and a profile were generated. Database identifiers are provided.

dency graphs, the fragments have been classified into three distinct classes on the basis of their frequency vectors. Two classes contain all fragments uniquely associated with the respective activity class, and a third class contains all remaining fragments. Edges in the dependency graphs are color-coded to reflect this classification scheme and permit the inspection of fragment pathways of subsets of molecules having similar activity.

4.2. DETECTION OF FRAGMENT HIERARCHIES

General Trends of Fragment Hierarchies

The graph representing all fragment dependencies for the fragment profile of the NK2-THR-ZINC set is shown in Figure 4.7. Root fragments at the top of the dependency graph, where pathways begin, are usually small and often single atoms like "C" (as in this case), "N", or "O". Such small fragments are common to most fragment populations but have differences in frequency. At the bottom of the graph, pathways end at individual molecules. Fragment pathways split at many tree levels and become increasingly specific for subsets of test molecules. As pathways proceed toward target molecules, fragments have the tendency to become larger in size and thus less generic and more specific.

Through color-coding it becomes evident that specific fractions of all fragment pathways are characteristic for subsets of molecules having similar activity. The NK2-THR-ZINC graph contains a total of 888 fragments. Only seven of the 888 fragments are produced by all 15 test molecules, and 182 fragments occur in all three molecule subsets, but not in all of their compounds. By contrast, 169 fragments (19.0%) are uniquely associated with activity class NK2 and 125 (14.1%) with class THR. Thus, about a third of all randomly generated fragments in this test set are activity class-unique. The observation that random MolBlaster profiles contain compound class-specific fragments is consistent with the findings reported in Section 4.1.1.

Class-Specific Subgraphs

Fragment pathways that are unique to NK2 and THR are shown in Figures 4.8 and 4.9, respectively. These subgraphs reveal how different dependency pathways converge on molecules belonging to an activity class. A noteworthy feature of these subgraphs is that their topology significantly differs. The NK2-specific fragment pathways show many more *hub* fragments that are conditional for the occurrence of many other fragments and therefore participate in various paths. This subgraph is compact and densely populated. By contrast, the THR subgraph in Figure 4.9 is sparsely populated and does not contain many hub fragments that are shared among active molecules. Consequently, the topology of ACCS subgraphs reflects intra-class structural homogeneity and molecular size. The average MACCS Tc value for pairwise comparison of the NK2 molecules is 0.55, and the corresponding average value for THR molecules is 0.43. NK2 molecules consist of on average 42.0 non-hydrogen atoms, respectively 29.6 for THR compounds. Therefore, structurally more similar and larger molecules such as NK2 produce more shared signature fragments and more densely connected subgraphs than structurally more diverse and smaller compounds such as THR (see also Figure 4.6).

For each activity class the class-specific subgraphs enable the classification of fragments according to their tree level. All ACCS that represent starting points of fragment pathways (and therefore do not depend on the occurrence of other ACCS) are designated *level 0* ACCS. Fragments that depend on *level 0* ACCS are called *level 1* ACCS, and so on.

CHAPTER 4. MINING FRAGMENT PROFILES

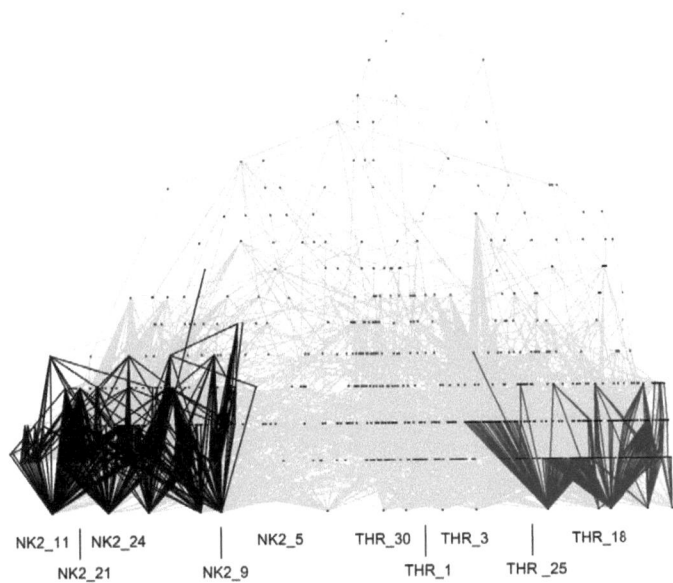

Fig. 4.7: **Dependency graph of a fragment profile.** The graph for the NK2-THR-ZINC fragment profile is shown. NK2 and THR-specific fragment pathways are colored black and dark gray, respectively. All other pathways are colored light gray.

Compound-Specific Pathways

A key feature of fragment hierarchies is that the subset of fragments unique to an activity class is organized in pathways that are specific for individual molecules. Table 4.4 summarizes a pathway that is specific for a NK2 molecule and reveals major characteristics. The pathway starts at the root level and extends over 10 fragments that co-occur in different compound classes or are class-unique. The frequency vectors shows that about half of these fragments are very narrowly distributed, and the bottom three fragments are NK2-unique. Clearly, the presence of class-unique fragments in fragment profiles helps to rationalize why these profiles could be successfully used for the identification of active compounds. This requires that class-unique fragments found in individual fragment populations are also selected for the class profile, which is accomplished by the sSE metric that selects fragments generated for all active compounds with comparable frequency. Given the PSE scoring method, a drawback of this approach has been that only the information content for one activity class is considered. In Table 4.4 the NK2-specific sSE values are also reported, that is the information content of fragments calculated only for the NK2 compound subset. The first four fragments in Table 4.4 all belong to the [0.95–1.0] sSE range for NK2, but are obviously not characteristic for this activity class. When PSE scoring is applied, widely distributed fragments like the ones mentioned above might favor the selection of false-positives, which was observed in Section 4.1. Dependency graphs enable the omission of generic fragments from class profiles, which is

4.2. DETECTION OF FRAGMENT HIERARCHIES 48

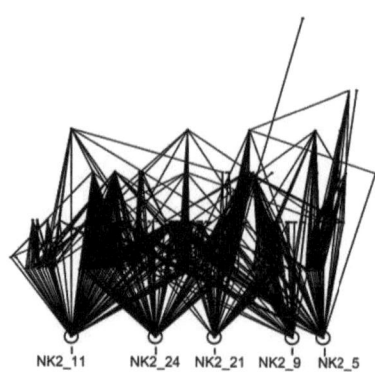

Fig. 4.8: NK2-specific fragment pathways. The NK2-specific subgraph is shown according to Figure 4.7. Terminal nodes at the bottom represent individual molecules.

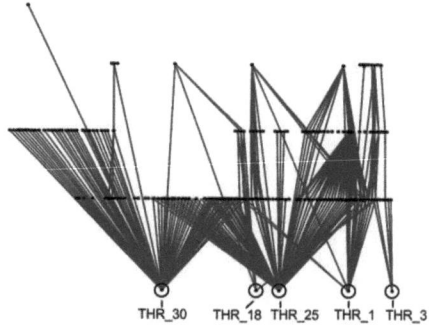

Fig. 4.9: THR-specific fragment pathways. The THR-specific subgraph is shown according to Figure 4.7. Terminal nodes at the bottom represent individual molecules. The NK2- and THR-specific subgraphs have distinct differences in topology, as discussed in the text.

expected to further increase the accuracy of database search calculations.

The observations discussed above demonstrate that random molecular fragment populations contain structural elements and hierarchies that have the character of molecular signatures. Two levels of signatures can be distinguished. First, combinations of unique fragments represent a compound class signature. Second, specific fragment pathways represent signatures of individual molecules within a class. Since multiple pathways exist for each molecule, they can also be combined to produce signature patterns.

fragment	frequency vector	sSE_{NK2}
C	(21 265, 26 335, 22 592, 21 147, 28 088, 16 443, 15 883, 16 876, 15 845, 13 144, 14 829, 15 427, 18 451, 18 408, 16 585)	0.996
CC	(3 602, 3 825, 3 108, 3 636, 3 573, 2 918, 2 627, 3 248, 2 667, 2 869, 1 817, 2 565, 2 716, 2 249, 3 103)	0.999
C=C	(1 396, 878, 936, 1 834, 1 724, 1 314, 865, 1 405, 790, 582, 666, 984, 1 282, 1 312, 992)	0.973
CCC	(336, 584, 351, 343, 433, 349, 479, 460, 551, 587, 240, 226, 334, 71, 118)	0.985
C/C=C/C	(34, 44, 23, 85, 55, 39, 72, 66, 50, 64, 64, 26, 65, 25, 22)	0.942
C=C(C)CC	(9, 5, 22, 10, 23, 22, 1, 23, 0, 0, 0, 4, 0, 0, 6)	0.911
NCCCC=C	(4, 2, 7, 5, 4, 0, 0, 4, 0, 0, 0, 0, 0, 0, 5)	0.956
N(C)CCCC=C	(4, 1, 3, 1, 4, 0, 0, 0, 0, 0, 0, 0, 0, 0, 0)	0.906
NCCNCCC	(0, 0, 3, 1, 4, 0, 0, 0, 0, 0, 0, 0, 0, 0, 0)	0.605
O=C[C@@H](NC)CC	(0, 0, 0, 1, 4, 0, 0, 0, 0, 0, 0, 0, 0, 0, 0)	0.311

Tab. 4.4: NK2 fragment pathway. Reported is a summary of a selected fragment pathway for molecule NK2_5 and NK2_9. SMILES strings of participating fragments are annotated with their corresponding frequency vectors. The first five frequency vector coordinates represent molecules from activity class NK2, the next five coordinates represent molecules from activity class THR, and the last five coordinates represent ZINC compounds. For each fragment the NK2-specific sSE value (sSE_{NK2}) is reported in order to correlate paths with different sSE ranges.

4.3 Similarity Searching using Activity Class Characteristic Substructures

In this section the utility of selected signature fragments as 2D descriptors for diverse activity classes is explored. Special attention is paid to the dependency relationships between fragments. It remained to be determined to what extent structural information is encoded in the hierarchical organization of activity-class characteristic fragment profiles. Therefore, fragments from different levels of the tree-like dependency graphs were analyzed for their class-specificity in virtual screening trials [67]. The analysis was complemented by a comparison to database search results calculated with standard reference methods.

4.3.1 Methodology for Similarity Searching

For the database search trials five high-throughput screening data sets available in PubChem were analyzed. These data sets included three screens for cathepsin B, L, and S cysteine protease inhibitors, a screen for JNK3 tyrosine kinase inhibitors, and another one for protein kinase A inhibitors. A summary is provided in Table 4.5. The experimental screening data sets were chosen because they consist not only of confirmed active but also confirmed inactive compounds and contain structurally diverse hits. Such hits provide challenging test cases for the analysis of structure-activity relationships. The structural diversity of active compounds in all five screening sets is reflected by low average pairwise Tanimoto similarity reported in Table 4.5 and can be further appreciated in Appendix C that shows representative examples of active compounds.

Generation of Activity-Class Characteristic Substructures

Considering the total number of hits available in each screening set, ten subsets of 11–16 active molecules were randomly taken from each set as reference molecules (see Table 4.5). Each reference set was fragmented together with 500 randomly selected ZINC compounds using 3 000 MolBlaster iterations with randomized numbers of deletions per step. For each reference set, the resulting fragment populations were used to determine cumulative numbers of ACCS for the top three levels (0, 1, 2) of their fragment trees. In Table 4.6, the average numbers of ACCS for all reference sets are reported. Independent of their biological activity, active reference molecules from each screening set consistently produced ACCS. At tree level 0, the average number of characteristic substructures ranged from 9.7 (CAB) to 36.5 (PKA). With the exception of PKA, cumulative numbers of ACCS at tree level 2 were always smaller than 100. Figure 4.10 shows representative ACCS examples for CAB. As can be seen, these substructures

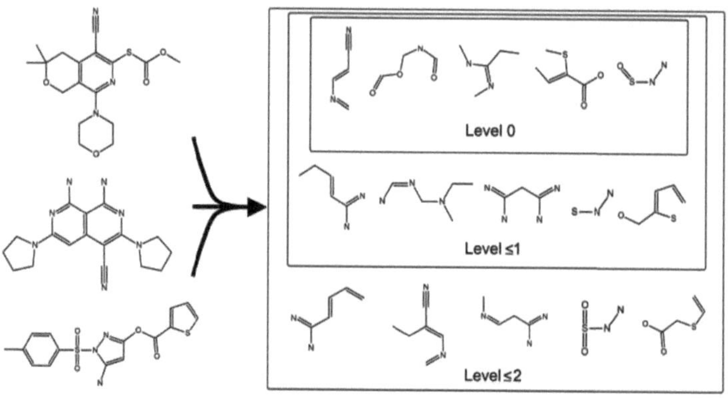

Fig. 4.10: Representative ACCS. An exemplary ACCS subset for the activity class CAB is shown. These substructures occur in fragment populations of a CAB reference set that includes the three compounds shown on the left. ACCS are classified according to their levels in fragment trees.

Code	Inhibitors	$N_{actives}$	Activity range	avg Tc	N_{ref}	$N_{inactives}$
CAB	Cathepsin B	36	46 nm–44 μm	0.45	12	63 287
CAL	Cathepsin L	49	3 nm–36 μm	0.43	16	57 764
CAS	Cathepsin S	34	4 nm–33 μm	0.54	12	61 723
JNK	JNK3	33	1 nm–15 μm	0.37	11	8 420
PKA	PKA	94	682 nm–357 μm	0.45	16	64 797

Tab. 4.5: Screening data sets. A summary of the screening data is provided. $N_{actives}$ is the number of hits per data set and IC_{50} values reports the activity range of these hits. $N_{inactives}$ gives the number of inactive screening set compounds and N_{ref} the number of active reference molecules used in similarity search calculations. The average Tanimoto coefficient (avg Tc) for pairwise comparison of hits is calculated using MACCS keys and reflects the structural heterogeneity of active compounds. All screening sets are publicly available in PubChem-Bioassays under the following AIDs: 453 (CAB); 460 (CAL); 501 (CAS); 530 (JNK); 524 (PKA).

are diverse and relatively small. Depending on the tree level, larger substructures can also be found.

Database Search Strategy

To investigate whether these substructures could be directly used to detect structure-activity relationships, ACCS for each reference set and tree level were encoded as binary keyed fingerprints, where each bit position detects the presence or absence of a class characteristic substructure. These small compound class-directed ACCS fingerprints (ACCS-FPs) were then used to search each screening data set for the remaining active molecules (that is, the total number of hits minus reference compounds). In these calculations, a nearest neighbor strategy was applied as a similarity search technique for multiple reference compounds [68]. Nearest neighbor methods separately calculate the similarity of a database compound to each individual reference molecule. Then either the largest similarity value is used, which is called the 1-NN strategy, or the similarity scores of k nearest neighbors are averaged (k-NN). The selection of the 3-NN search strategy was motivated by the characteristics of ACCS. According to their definition, ACCS encode structural information for at least two active molecules. Furthermore, ACCS pathways become increasingly specific for a subset of active compounds. Taken together, 3-NN calculations on the basis of Tanimoto similarity was appropriate to analyze the predictive ability of ACCS-FPs for a compound set, rather than individual molecules.

4.3.2 Analysis of Similarity Search Results

Table 4.6 reports average hit rates for ACCS-FPs for the first three tree levels and the different screening data sets. ACCS-FPs consistently retrieved active molecules and displayed a strong tendency to enrich hits in small selection sets of 5 compounds. Moreover, the majority of selection sets of 50 compounds contained about 10%–20% active molecules. A graphical representation of search performance is provided in Figure 4.11, which shows hit rate maps for

4.3. SIMILARITY SEARCHING USING FRAGMENT HIERARCHIES

CAB as an example. These graphs monitor hit rates over all tree levels and reveal that ACCS-FPs containing fragments of the first few tree levels already displayed top search performance. Even the smallest ACCS-FPs consisting only of substructures identified at tree level 0 produced hit rates comparable to those of larger versions of ACCS-FPs. Their search performance was not dominated by large fragments. At tree level 0, removal of fragments larger than 50% of the average size (number of atoms) of reference molecules typically reduced ACCS sets by less than 10% and did not notably change search performance. This indicates that fragments are usually small and emphasized the importance of ACCS combinations for the prediction of structure-activity relationships, rather than individual fragments. ACCS at tree level 0 represent starting points of class-specific fragment pathways and thus occur independently of each other. The observation that the addition of dependent fragments at tree levels 1 and 2 did not significantly increase search performance, indicated that combinations of ACCS at origins of fragment pathways captured much class-specific information.

Moreover, the addition of dependent fragments at increasing tree levels can produce substructure combinations that are not represented by individual reference molecules. The use of such combinations is likely to increase the probability of detecting other database compounds. For example, Figure 3 shows that hit rates for CAB decreased when substructures up to tree

Activity class	Tree level	ACCS	HR_5	HR_{50}	HR_{100}
CAB	0	9.7	0.58	0.08	0.04
	≤ 1	33.9	0.69	0.10	0.05
	≤ 2	49.14	0.69	0.09	0.05
CAL	0	25.7	0.24	0.06	0.03
	≤ 1	69.3	0.22	0.06	0.04
	≤ 2	93.9	0.26	0.07	0.04
CAS	0	21.2	0.84	0.19	0.11
	≤ 1	50.1	0.80	0.19	0.11
	≤ 2	82.5	0.78	0.19	0.10
JNK	0	25.6	0.38	0.09	0.05
	≤ 1	47.9	0.36	0.09	0.05
	≤ 2	59.6	0.31	0.08	0.05
PKA	0	36.5	0.52	0.11	0.08
	≤ 1	99.4	0.40	0.10	0.10
	≤ 2	156.5	0.34	0.11	0.11

Tab. 4.6: ACCS and average hit rates of ACCS-FPs. For each screening data set, average numbers of ACCS in reference sets are reported at different tree levels. Also reported are average hit rates (HR) for similarity searching using ACCS fingerprints. For each of ten reference sets, independent search calculations were carried out. Hit rates were calculated for the top-ranked five, 50, and 100 screening set molecules on the basis of Tanimoto similarity.

CHAPTER 4. MINING FRAGMENT PROFILES

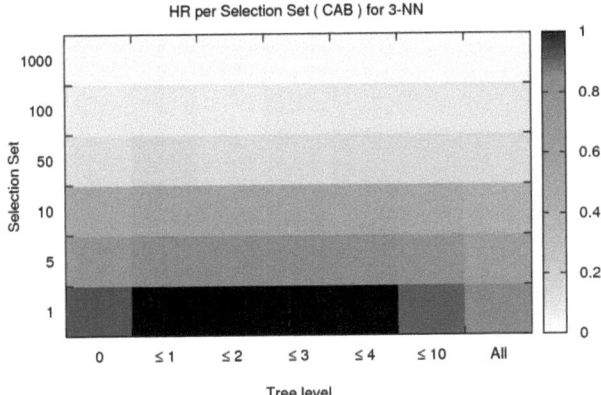

Fig. 4.11: Hit rate map for activity class CAB. Average hit rates are reported for substructure combinations at different tree levels. Hit rates are color-coded using a continuous spectrum from black (hit rate 1.0, that is 100%) to white (hit rate 0.0).

level 10 were added. Therefore, it is not required to consider all ACCS produced by a reference set. On the contrary, combinations of small subsets of ACCS from different class-specific pathways were found to encode sufficient information and could be used to represent larger sets of redundant fragments.

Scaffold Hopping Potential

To analyze the quality of the similarity search results the number of unique scaffolds in correctly identified active hits were determined. The results are reported in Table 4.7 and reveal that ACCS-FP calculation displayed a clear tendency to detect diverse scaffolds. A noteworthy observation is that for small selection set sizes, ACCS of level zero detected at least as many unique scaffolds as higher level ACCS-FPs, and often more. This observation further emphasizes that fragments from low dependency levels encode much class-specific information, while the addition of fragments from higher levels increases the focus of the ACCS-FP on a subset of active compounds. Taken together, the results demonstrate that class-specific combinations of defined random fragments encoded in ACCS-FPs have the potential to recognize structurally diverse compounds.

Reference Calculations

For all reference sets 3-NN calculations were carried out on the basis of Tanimoto similarity with MACCS (166 bits), the TGD fingerprint (420 bits), TGT (1 704 bits) and Molprint 2D. TGD is an atom pair type fingerprint recording pairs of seven atom types over a maximum path length of 15 bonds. TGT is a three-point pharmacophore-type 2D fingerprint that captures triangles of four atomic features using graph distances divided into six distance ranges. Molprint 2D generates layered atom environments and varying numbers of strings per molecule.

4.3. SIMILARITY SEARCHING USING FRAGMENT HIERARCHIES

Activity class	Tree level	Top 5	Top 50	Top 100
CAB	0	1.5 (2.9)	1.9 (4.1)	2.2 (4.4)
	≤1	1.4 (3.4)	2.2 (5.0)	2.4 (5.2)
	≤2	1.4 (3.4)	1.9 (4.3)	2.1 (4.7)
CAL	0	1.0 (1.2)	2.4 (3.0)	2.4 (3.0)
	≤1	0.9 (1.1)	2.5 (3.1)	3.1 (3.8)
	≤2	1.0 (1.3)	2.8 (3.4)	3.3 (4.2)
CAS	0	2.3 (4.2)	7.4 (9.7)	8.3 (10.6)
	≤1	2.1 (4.0)	7.2 (9.5)	8.3 (10.6)
	≤2	2.2 (3.9)	7.3 (9.5)	8.0 (10.4)
JNK	0	1.1 (1.9)	2.7 (4.5)	3.3 (5.4)
	≤1	0.9 (1.8)	2.9 (4.5)	3.0 (4.7)
	≤2	1.0 (1.6)	2.0 (4.0)	3.0 (4.7)
PKA	0	2.1 (5.0)	4.4 (19.9)	6.7 (19.9)
	≤1	1.5 (2.6)	4.2 (5.5)	7.5 (8.3)
	≤2	1.2 (1.7)	4.4 (5.7)	8.0 (10.6)

Tab. 4.7: Distinct scaffolds. For all similarity search trials according to Table 4.6 the average number of distinct scaffolds representing the hits is reported. For each selection set, the average number of correctly identified hits is given in parentheses.

Table 4.8 reports the results of corresponding similarity search calculations using these four different fingerprints. As already observed in Chapter 3, differences in hit rates between the diverse fingerprint representations were subtle. ACCS-FPs derived from level 0 performed best for two of the five screening sets, and for the other three sets fingerprint search performance maximally differed by approximately 20%. For small selection sets, ACCS-FPs produced consistently higher hit rates than the MACCS keys and the TGD fingerprint. TGT achieved a few percent higher hit rates in three cases, but failed to detect active protein kinase inhibitors (PKA). In comparison with Molprint 2D, the ACCS-FPs performed better in three of five cases, although differences were marginal. For larger selection set sizes, the performance of all five fingerprint representations were comparable.

The results in Table 4.6 and Table 4.8 show that ACCS-FP search performance compared favorably to other 2D fingerprints. At tree level 0, ACCS-FPs contain on average about 24 substructures and are thus even smaller in size than so-called mini-fingerprints (MFPs), which were introduced several years ago as hybrid fingerprints consisting of selected MACCS keys and property descriptors [64]. MFPs have a minimum number of about 60 bit positions and have thus far been the smallest 2D fingerprints.

Activity class	Fingerprint	HR_5	HR_{50}	HR_{100}
CAB	MACCS	0.52	0.11	0.05
	TGD	0.52	0.09	0.05
	TGT	0.66	0.08	0.04
	Molprint 2D	0.76	0.13	0.07
	ACCS 0	0.58	0.08	0.04
CAL	MACCS	0.08	0.02	0.01
	TGD	0.18	0.06	0.04
	TGT	0.30	0.06	0.03
	Molprint 2D	0.30	0.09	0.05
	ACCS 0	0.24	0.06	0.03
CAS	MACCS	0.54	0.19	0.10
	TGD	0.34	0.07	0.05
	TGT	0.38	0.08	0.04
	Molprint 2D	0.74	0.20	0.11
	ACCS 0	0.84	0.19	0.11
JNK	MACCS	0.50	0.11	0.07
	TGD	0.36	0.05	0.04
	TGT	0.56	0.08	0.04
	Molprint 2D	0.34	0.16	0.10
	ACCS 0	0.38	0.09	0.05
PKA	MACCS	0.12	0.05	0.04
	TGD	0.28	0.08	0.05
	TGT	0.10	0.04	0.02
	Molprint 2D	0.48	0.25	0.18
	ACCS 0	0.52	0.11	0.08

Tab. 4.8: **Average hit rates for reference calculations.** Reported are average hit rates for reference calculations using MACCS keys, TGD, TGT, and Molprint 2D fingerprints, presented according to Table 4.6. For comparison average hit rates achieved with ACCS-FPs extracted from tree level 0 are also shown.

4.4 Conclusion

In this chapter it is shown that randomly generated fragments can be organized according to their dependency of occurrence in individual fragment populations of a defined compound set. The dependency relationships between fragments form a hierarchical, tree-like structure of fragment profiles where fragments are organized in pathways that are specific for individual molecules. A key feature of the approach introduced herein is that for a set of active compounds specific signature fragments can be extracted that are not present in the fragment background of the screening database. These fragments are called *Activity Class Characteristic Substructures* (ACCS). Furthermore, from compound class-specific fragment pathways, specific combinations of substructures can be derived. The smallest possible ACCS set was collected from level 0 in

4.4. CONCLUSION

the corresponding fragment tree, which represents the most generic fragmentation level. It was found that fragments at higher levels become larger in size and increasingly compound-specific. ACCS-FPs are introduced as prototypic fingerprint representations of ACCS combinations. In virtual screening trials, combinations of only $\sim$20 ACCS successfully detect different structure-activity relationships. In addition to their small size, characteristic features of ACCS-FPs include that they are compound class-directed and highly variable in composition. Thus, it can be concluded that random fragment populations are a valuable source for the identification of substructure combinations that are signatures of different compound classes. Such substructure combinations provide a basis for the development of class-specific 2D similarity search tools.

Chapter 5

Distribution and Origin of ACCS in Compound Sets

In order to better understand the high performance of small ACCS-FPs in similarity searching, a systematic analysis of the ACCS distribution in activity classes and large background databases is carried out. Additional, the structural origin of ACCS within parent compounds is analyzed in order to identify molecular substructures that account for the generation of signature fragments.

Analysis of the distribution of ACCS within active and database compounds is reported in Section 5.1. In addition to the occurrence of individual ACCS, their combination were analyzed. In Section 5.2 a systematic mapping of ACCS to their source molecules is performed to identify molecular substructures produced by ACCS overlap, so-called *cores*. After the introduction of the fragment mapping methodology in Subsection 5.2.1, these cores are characterized as origin of ACCS in Subsection 5.2.2. Finally, in Subsection 5.2.3 the structural meaning of fragment hierarchies is explored.

5.1 Distribution of ACCS in Diverse Compound Sets

In order to elucidate potential reasons for the high predictive potential of ACCS, their distribution in active and database compounds and their information content were further explored. Specifically, the analysis aimed at understanding why limited numbers of small random fragments were capable to account for diverse structure-activity relationships.

5.1.1 Methodology

The compound sets used in this study were specifically designed to be of increasing intra-class structural diversity [69]. Table 5.1 summarizes these compound sets. Each set was fragmented with 3 000 MolBlaster iterations together with a background set of 500 compounds that were arbitrarily taken from ZINC. For each activity class, only the ACCS set from level 0 was

5.1. DISTRIBUTION OF ACCS

Code	Biological activity	$N_{actives}$	avg Tc	dev	N_{ACCS}
ARI	aldose reductase inhibitors	23	0.327	0.157	70
CAB	cathepsin B inhibitors	36	0.450	0.161	71
ETA	endothelin antagonists	22	0.396	0.140	70

Tab. 5.1: Compound activity classes. The molecule set CAB is available in PubChem-Bioassays (AID: 453). The other sets were taken from Tovar et al. [69] and were originally assembled from the MDDR. $N_{actives}$ reports the number of compounds per set and N_{ACCS} the number of level 0 ACCS generated from them. The average MACCS Tanimoto coefficient value (avg Tc) for pairwise compound comparison and the corresponding standard deviation (dev) reflect the degree of intra-class structural diversity. According to the classification by Tovar et al., the compound set ARI shows high, ETA medium, and CAB low heterogeneity.

extracted from the corresponding fragment tree, since these fragments contained most basic compound class information. The derived ACCS sets were searched as substructures against the individual activity classes as well as the ZINC database consisting of ~3.7 million molecules. The database molecules were assumed to be inactive, although for some compounds this may not be the case, as discussed below.

5.1.2 Evaluation

Table 5.1 shows that the activity classes with 22 to 36 molecules generated 70 and 71 level 0 ACCS, respectively, regardless of intra-class diversity. However, the size of the complete ACCS set varied significantly, as further explained below. In Figure 5.1, the distribution of ACCS for known active and ZINC database compounds is reported. The results revealed that ACCS were heterogeneously distributed for both sets.

For active compounds 18–26% of the molecules only contained a small number of ACCS, if any. The most diverse set (ARI) contained compounds matching no ACCS (8.7%). These molecules are structural outliers of this class and do not contribute any fragment to the ACCS set. Nevertheless, the number of outliers within these classes is small and one can detect a tendency of active compounds to match large numbers of ACCS.

In Figure 5.1, the most striking observation is that for the major part of all database compounds no single ACCS was found. Although ACCS were generated against a background of only 500 ZINC compounds, more than three million ZINC compounds did not contain any ACCS for the three different activity classes. Moreover, the number of ZINC compounds containing multiple ACCS diminished rapidly with increasing ACCS numbers. As an example, the detailed distribution of ACCS for activity class ETA is shown in Table 5.2. The data for the other sets are provided in Appendix D and display equivalent trends. The level 0 ACCS set generated for ETA consisted of a total of 70 substructures, but no individual ETA molecule was found to contain more than 19 ACCS. This can be rationalized by the tree-like dependency hierarchy of fragments, when ACCS from level 0 represent starting points for

CHAPTER 5. DISTRIBUTION AND ORIGIN OF ACCS 59

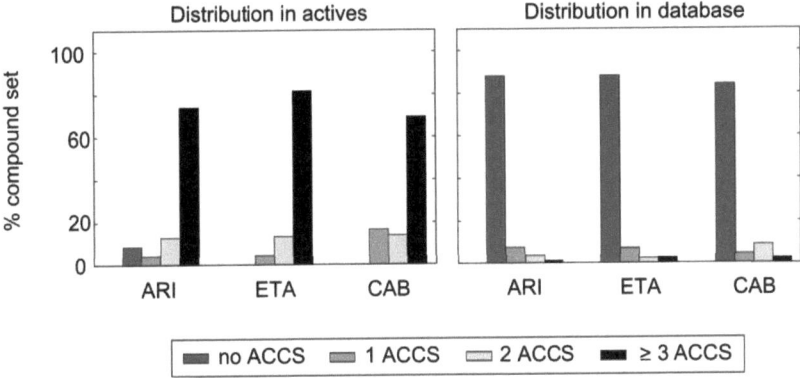

Fig. 5.1: **Distributions of ACCS in diverse compound sets.** The percentage of compounds matched by ACCS derived from ARI, ETA and CAB is reported. On the left side the distribution of ACCS in active compounds is given and on the right in the ZINC database. For comparison, the percentage of compounds matching no ACCS (dark gray columns), only one ACCS (medium gray), two ACCS (light gray) or at least three ACCS (black) is shown.

compound-specific pathways. If at all, only a subset of ACCS leads to all active molecules and therefore complete ACCS sets are rarely found in test compounds. Thus, each active compound is typically characterized by a specific subset of ACCS.

The number of ACCS present in individual active molecules varied in part significantly. For example, four ETA compounds contained one or two ACCS, and 13 compounds contained nine to 19 ACCS. Eleven ZINC compounds were found to contain 20 or 21 ETA-ACCS and thus more than any of the known actives. These database compounds would represent prime candidates for the evaluation of activity because they contain the most class-characteristic fragments. In Figure 5.2, the three compounds with 21 ETA ACCS are shown in combination with a known active compound containing 19 ACCS. One of these ZINC compounds indeed is labeled as endothelin antagonist, which underlines the predictive utility of ACCS combinations.

To go a step further, the presence or absence of class-specific ACCS combinations in database compounds was systematically assessed. For this purpose, ACCS combinations of each active compound were searched against the database and the number of exact matches was recorded. The results of this analysis is reported in Table 5.3. It is observed that only a minor fraction of 3.7 million ZINC molecules (0.05%–0.75%) matched unique combinations of more than two ACCS found in active compounds. Simply selecting molecules from the database that shared a specific combination of at least seven ACCS with active compounds would have recovered 12 of 23 ARI compounds together with 1210 ZINC molecules, 14 of 22 ETA compounds with only 104 ZINC molecules, and 15 of 36 CAB actives with 317 ZINC molecules. In contrast to ZINC, combinations of multiple ACCS were fairly evenly distributed over the activity class.

Thus, combinations of multiple ACCS were highly specific for subsets of active compounds.

In summary, these findings rationalize the predictive utility of ACCS combinations and the high performance of small ACCS fingerprints observed in similarity searching. Many activity-class characteristic substructures are rarely found in database compounds and, moreover, combinations of multiple ACCS become highly discriminatory and a signature of active compounds.

5.2 Origin of ACCS in Active Compounds

In order to determine the origin of ACCS in active compounds and better understand their structural meaning, ACCS were systematically mapped on their source molecules [70].

5.2.1 Molecular Mapping

A total of 1 025 compounds from 45 different activity classes of varying diversity was systematically analyzed. For each test molecule, random fragment populations were generated using MolBlaster and the same fragmentation protocol applied for the virtual screening trials in Chap-

N_{ACCS}	N_{AC}	N_{DB}
0	0	3 243 075
1	1	265 072
2	3	82 407
3	1	15 876
4	2	46 730
5	0	8 823
6	1	6 169
7	0	7 886
8	1	4 427
9	4	1 334
10	1	895
11	0	732
12	0	365
13	0	437
14	1	70
15	0	31
16	0	30
17	1	33
18	4	24
19	2	16
20	0	8
21	0	3

Tab. 5.2: ACCS distribution for ETA. Reported are the number of active (N_{AC}) and ZINC database compounds (N_{DB}) that contain a certain number of ACCS (N_{ACCS}). No compound was found having more than 21 ETA-ACCS.

	ARI			ETA			CAB	
N_{ACCS}	N_{AC}	N_{DB}	N_{ACCS}	N_{AC}	N_{DB}	N_{ACCS}	N_{AC}	N_{DB}
1	1	32 480	1	1	9 702	1	6	20 123
2	3	8 433	2	3	8 809	2	5	283 210
3	2	50	3	1	96	3	3	1 609
4	1	2	4	2	27 870	4	3	15
6	2	9 667	6	1	0	5	2	53
7	1	7	8	1	0	6	2	2
8	1	1	9	4	71	8	3	7
9	1	1	10	1	7	9	2	18
10	2	1 112	14	1	2	10	4	4
11	1	2	17	1	1	12	1	10
12	2	20	18	4	21	13	1	157
13	1	26	19	2	2	14	2	76
14	2	37				15	1	43
15	1	4				16	1	2

Tab. 5.3: Distributions of unique ACCS combinations. Reported are the number of active (N_{AC}) and ZINC database compounds (N_{DB}) that contain unique combinations of increasing numbers of ACCS (N_{ACCS}) for the activity classes ARI, ETA, and CAB.

ter 4. For each activity class, a set of 500 randomly selected ZINC compounds was used as a structural background to identify ACCS. Up to six different background sets were employed in these calculations in order to study the influence of background molecules on the composition of ACCS sets. The ACCS were mapped on active molecules by performing a subgraph search for each fragment. Whenever a fragment matched an atom of a test molecule, a counter for the matched atom was increased by one. For each atom, division of its final counter state by the total number of matched substructures gave its *match rate*. For each active molecule, alternative core regions, $core_x$, were defined as the set of all atoms of the molecule that have an ACCS match rate greater than $x\%$ (with x referred to as the core level). Hence, for each molecule maximal 10 cores ($core_{90}$ to $core_0$) could be detected. The mapping procedure is illustrated in Figure 5.3.

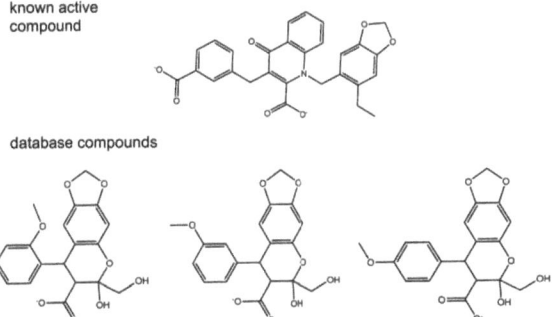

Fig. 5.2: Exemplary compounds with different numbers of ACCS keys. Shown at the top is a known ETA compound that is matched by 19 ACCS. At the bottom, three ZINC compounds are shown that contain 21 ACCS. The compound in the center is a known endothelin antagonist available in ZINC.

5.2. ORIGIN OF ACCS

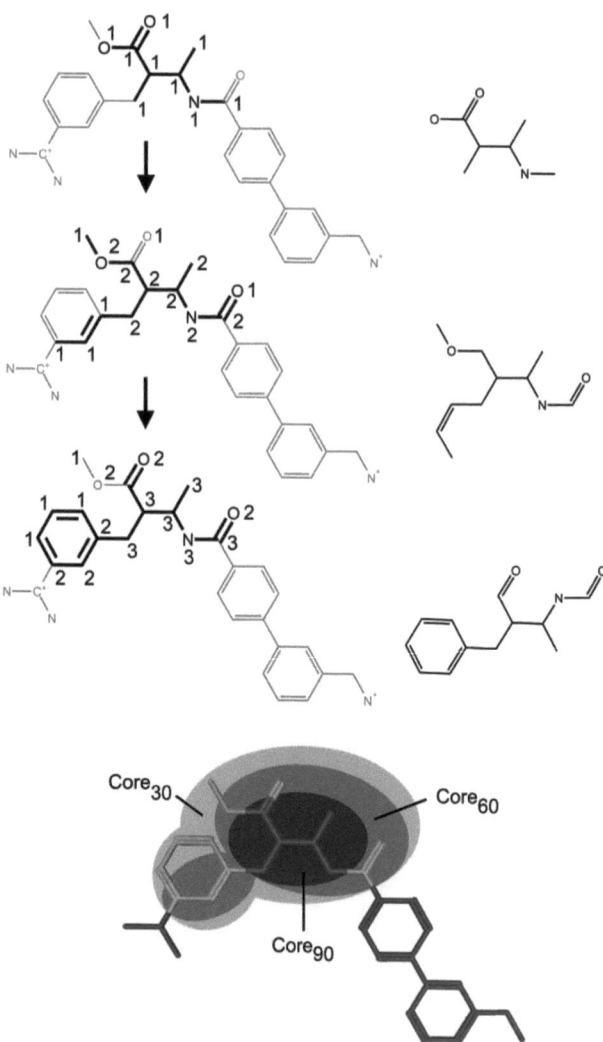

Fig. 5.3: Substructure mapping and core derivation. The procedure of iterative ACCS mapping is illustrated for a hypothetical ACCS set consisting of three fragments. Each fragment is mapped onto the 2D graph of the test molecule and the atom count for matched atoms is updated after each step. Finally, the division of the counter by the total number of matched substructures gives the atom match rate for each atom of the molecule. In this example, three distinct cores can be distinguished (according to the background color): $core_{90}$ (dark grey), $core_{60}$ (dark and medium grey), and $core_{30}$ (dark, medium, light grey). Parts of the molecule that were not matched have no backround color.

5.2.2 Observations for Molecular Mapping

After fragment mapping 93% of the active molecules formed a core and more than 60% showed a core$_{90}$. Furthermore, all molecules forming cores did so at the core$_{40}$ level at for latest. As an example, the core$_{70}$ for serotonin (5-HT) receptor ligands are depicted in Figure 5.4. The major part (79%) of all actives only have a single core that exclusively grows through the addition of atoms that are directly bonded to core atoms. Distinct cores within one molecule were only very rarely seen. These observation led to the conclusion that cores shared by most active compounds of a class (e.g., core$_{90}$–core$_{70}$) represent small regions of recurrent structural patterns. Furthermore, regions of fragment overlap were not scattered over molecules, but formed coherent cores. Changing the ZINC background sets that were co-fragmented with active compounds led to very little variation of maximally 5% in ACCS-dependent core formation. Thus, the distribution of characteristic substructures was not sensitive to the composition of randomly chosen background database molecules. These observations provided strong evidence for class-specific core formation in different sets of active compounds.

5.2.3 Structural Meaning of Fragment Hierarchies

In the light of these findings the structural meaning of fragment dependency hierarchies was further analyzed. For the activity classes used in Section 5.1, the corresponding ACCS and their hierarchical organization were calculated. The complete ACCS sets were used to determine the individual cores for each molecule, especially the most stringent core (termed core$_{MS}$) and

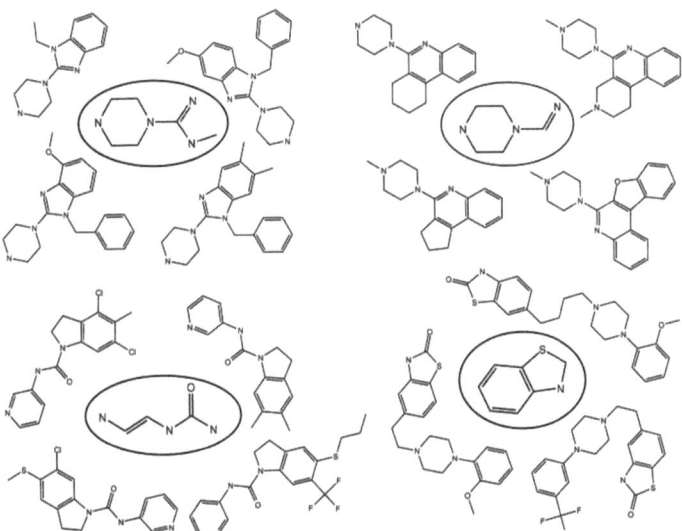

Fig. 5.4: Exemplary cores for 5-HT receptor ligands. The core$_{70}$ of four clusters is circled and surrounded by examples of molecules belonging to these clusters.

the core$_{40}$. Here, core$_{MS}$ reflects the most class-specific patterns that are shared by active compounds, while core$_{40}$ mirror the least common molecular substructures from which ACCS were derived. Then level 0 ACCS were mapped to the compounds in order to investigate their overlap with these cores. The results are reported in Table 5.4. It was found that level 0 ACCS mapped the core$_{MS}$ to at least 95%, indicating that these small sets of fragments are a signature for the class-specific structural patterns. The larger core$_{40}$ can not be completely matched by level 0 ACCS. These unmatched molecular substructures are the origin of ACCS from higher dependency levels and therefore increasingly compound-specific. Hence, the hierarchical organization of ACCS corresponds to a gradient of structural resemblance within an activity class. Starting from level 0, ACCS describe patterns that are most generic for an activity class. Additional fragments from higher dependency levels complement these patterns and render them more compound-specific. This view is fully consistent with the ability of level 0 ACCS to represent the corresponding complete ACCS sets.

Code	N_{ACCS}	$N_{ACCS\ L0}$	core$_{MS}$ overlap (%)	core$_{40}$ overlap (%)
ARI	623	70	95.45	84.62
CAB	2 228	71	98.86	89.98
ETA	799	70	96.86	82.53

Tab. 5.4: Mapping of level 0 ACCS to cores substructures. For each molecule of the activity classes in Table 5.1 the most stringent core (core$_{MS}$) and core$_{40}$ are calculated. The overlap of these cores by ACCS from level 0 is reported. For comparison, the total number of ACCS (N_{ACCS}) and the number of level 0 ACCS ($N_{ACCS\ L0}$) is shown.

5.3 Summary and Conclusions

The first section reveals an uneven distribution of ACCS among active compounds and (assumed inactive) database compounds. It was observed that active compounds have a tendency to map many of these substructures. In contrast, ACCS can not be found for the majority of database compounds. Moreover, the number of database compounds sharing combinations of ACCS diminishes rapidly, whereas the presence of multiple ACCS is fairly evenly distributed over active compounds, thus making ACCS combinations highly discriminatory for an activity class.

In the second part it is found that fragment combinations that are statistical signatures of compound classes have a defined structural meaning: they form well-defined common cores in active molecules. These cores are in general stable when increasingly compound-specific fragments are mapped to the molecules. Core regions correlate with molecular substructures of high fragment overlap and therefore represent structural patterns that are characteristic for a subset of active compounds. These findings demonstrate that random fragment populations encode specific structural information and rationalize the emergence of fragment dependency relationships.

Chapter 6
Summary and Conclusions

In the introductory chapter three central question were formulated that guided the studies presented in this thesis. A major goal was to analyze randomly generated fragment populations, explore their intrinsic information content, and evaluate their potential to represent molecular structure-activity relationships. This thesis introduces several novel methods for the generation, evaluation, and application of random fragment populations and many conclusions were drawn from these studies. This final chapter summarizes substantial findings.

Question 1: Can randomly generated fragments be used for the assessment of molecular similarity relationships?

To answer this question the *MolBlaster* fragmentation method was designed and implemented. Molecular fragmentation is achieved by random deletion of rows from connectivity tables of 2D graph representations, which corresponds to breaking bonds in a molecule. Basic parameters of this method includes the number of bond deletions carried out during each fragmentation step and the number of iterations. It was demonstrated that randomizing the number of bond deletion produces fragment populations with high information content, irrespective to the topological complexity of the underlying molecular graphs. Furthermore, it was shown that 2 000 MolBlaster iterations are sufficient to produce stable fragment populations.

Initial comparisons of fragment populations suggest their utility to detect structural resemblance of compounds. For the analysis and comparison of fragment populations, the entropy-based similarity metric $rDSE$ was introduced that correctly differentiates similarity relationships of varying degrees.

In virtual screening trials, fragment profiles are found to display significant specificity for the detection of structure-activity relationships. Activity-class characteristic fragment profiles are generated through selection of substructures with high information content for the set of active compounds. Another novel entropy-based scoring metric termed PSE was designed that takes the class-specificity of fragments into account. For virtual screening trials, PSE-based recovery rates are comparable to state-of-the-art 2D fingerprint representations. Correctly identified hits are typically enriched among the highest-scored compounds and often show core structures different from the reference molecules, indicating the potential of fragment profiles to aid in scaffold hopping.

As a result, random fragment populations are found to encode sufficient chemical information to mirror molecular similarity relationships.

Question 2: Can signature substructures be identified from randomly generated fragment profiles that are characteristic for individual activity classes?

Systematic determination of conditional probabilities of fragment co-occurrence in diverse compounds provides a conceptual framework to quantify dependency relationships between pairs of fragments. These dependency relationships lead to a hierarchical, tree-like organization of fragment profiles where individual fragments are arranged in compound-specific pathways. Such pathways become increasingly specific for single compounds. When biological activity of test molecules is considered, subgraphs of so-called *Activity Class Characteristic Substructures* (ACCS) can be extracted from hierarchical fragment trees. Taking advantage of the classification of ACCS into different tree levels, ACCS-FPs of varying size were introduced as prototypic fingerprint representations. In virtual screening trials, approximately 20 ACCS derived from tree level 0 are sufficient to detect structure-activity relationships. In systematic similarity search calculations, ACCS-FPs meet or exceed the performance of state-of-the-art 2D fingerprints of larger size and much higher complexity. These findings are rationalized by the signature character of ACCS. Thus, random fragment populations prove to be a valuable source for the identification of structural signatures for different compound classes. Such signatures are identified through systematic evaluation of fragment co-occurrence in active compounds.

Question 3: How can the predictive utility of randomly generated fragments be rationalized?

The distribution of ACCS in active and database compounds was systematically analyzed. It was shown that active compounds display the tendency to contain many of ACCS, whereas database compounds match few, if any. Moreover, the number of database compounds matching ACCS diminishes rapidly. By contrast, ACCS are evenly distributed in active compounds. A key finding is that ACCS combinations taken from fragment pathway are highly specific for active compounds and very rarely occur in database molecules.

Systematic mapping of ACCS combinations on source molecules reveals that ACCS typically originate from coherent molecular core regions.

Taken together, the studies in this thesis demonstrate for the first time that randomly generated fragments contain molecular signatures and highly class-specific fragment combinations that can be utilized for the successful exploration of diverse structure-activity relationships.

Appendix A

Software and Databases

Software and databases used in this thesis are listed below, in alphabetic order.

Software

Daylight	Daylight toolkit
Description:	Programming library for computational chemical information processing. Enables fingerprinting of molecules.
Developer:	Daylight Chemical Information System Inc, Aliso Viejo, CA (USA)
URL:	http://www.daylight.com/products/toolkit.html
Graphviz	Graph Visualization Software
Description:	Open source tool to display and manipulate large graphs.
Developer:	AT&T Research Labs, Florham Park, NJ (USA)
References:	Emden et al. [71]
URL:	http://graphviz.org/
MOE	Molecular Operating Environment
Description:	Research software for computational chemistry. Integrates tools for computer-assisted drug discovery, e.g. custom fingerprints systems are supported.
Developer:	Chemical Computing Group, Montreal (Canada)
URL:	http://www.chemcomp.com/

Databases

CMC	
Description:	The Comprehensive Medicinal Chemistry Database (Version 99.1) contains 8,400 pharmaceutical compounds and provides important biochemical properties of stored molecules.
Provider:	MDL Information Systems Inc, San Leandro, CA (USA)
URL:	http://www.mdl.com/products/knowledge/medicinal_chem/

MDDR	
Description:	The MDL Drug Data Report (MDDR) contains ~160,000 biologically active compounds that cover the patent literature, journals, meetings and congresses.
Provider:	MDL Information Systems Inc, San Leandro, CA (USA)
URL:	http://www.mdl.com/products/knowledge/drug_data_report/

PubChem	
Description:	The Pubchem BioAssay database provides bioactivity results from more than thousand high-throughput screening programs with several million structures.
Provider:	National Center for Biotechnology Information (NCBI), Bethesda, MD (USA)
URL:	http://www.ncbi.nlm.nih.gov/sites/entrez?db=pcassay

ZINC	
Description:	Database of ~5.6 million compounds collected from vendor catalogs. Contains multiple conformations and tautomeric forms. In this thesis, a filtered version of ~3.7 unique molecules is used.
Provider:	Shoichet Laboratory, UCSF, San Francisco, CA (USA)
References:	Irwin et al. [72]
URL:	http://zinc.docking.org/

Appendix B

Mining Frequently Occurring Fragments

In Chapter 4 the sSE range-dependence of fragment distributions was analyzed, and results were reported for four of 15 activity classes used in virtual screening trials. In Table B.1 the results for the remaining 11 activity classes are provided.

Table B.1: Size and Composition of Fragment Sets.

For each activity class, the average number of fragments (avg no. frgmts) for specified sSE ranges is reported. Respectively, the percentage of fragments belonging to the set of most frequently occurring fragments (% freq set) is also shown. The most frequent fragments are those that occur in at least 10 000 compounds of the used ZINC background database.

sSE range	avg no. frgmts	% freq set	avg no. frgmts	% freq set	avg no frgmts	% freq set
	AA2		ANA		CAE	
[0.95–1.0]	6.6	100	39.8	79.8	18.4	54.9
[0.90–1.0]	11.6	99.6	98.5	50.5	24.9	51.0
[0.85–1.0]	20.2	97.1	164.7	34.4	33.2	50.4
[0.80–1.0]	30.3	92.1	236.4	26.8	45.0	44.6
[0.75–1.0]	41.9	84.0	309.9	22.3	52.3	44.1
	CAL		DD1		ESU	
[0.95–1.0]	18.1	95.8	19.4	92.5	28.2	58.9
[0.90–1.0]	36.1	91.0	39.9	79.3	60.9	47.1
[0.85–1.0]	57.3	81.5	59.4	66.9	94.1	40.9
[0.80–1.0]	76.5	71.9	79.6	59.4	123.6	37.1
[0.75–1.0]	116.7	57.8	100.5	52.5	150.6	32.7
	HIV		KAP		KRA	
[0.95–1.0]	67.7	59.6	16.1	96.5	13.0	95.2
[0.90–1.0]	93.3	50.5	34.5	90.8	23.3	86.1
[0.85–1.0]	144.8	40.7	54.0	80.6	39.5	76.4
[0.80–1.0]	175.0	35.8	73.9	69.5	56.6	67.9
[0.75–1.0]	212.8	31.4	91.0	61.8	79.6	58.9
	LAC		SQS			
[0.95–1.0]	6.9	99.3	9.5	100		
[0.90–1.0]	15.7	96.6	20.3	96.8		
[0.85–1.0]	26.5	93.8	38.6	88.4		
[0.80–1.0]	37.6	88.8	54.0	77.4		
[0.75–1.0]	53.3	80.7	67.5	67.8		

Tab. B.1: Size and Composition of Fragment Sets.

Appendix C

Screening Dataset

In Chapter 4 five high-throughput screening data sets obtained from PubChem were used for virtual screening calculations. Known active compounds were used to generate a set of ACCS. In Figure C.1 representative active compounds for each activity class are illustrated.

Figure C.1: Representative active compounds.

For each screening data set used in virtual screening trials, three randomly selected active molecules are shown.

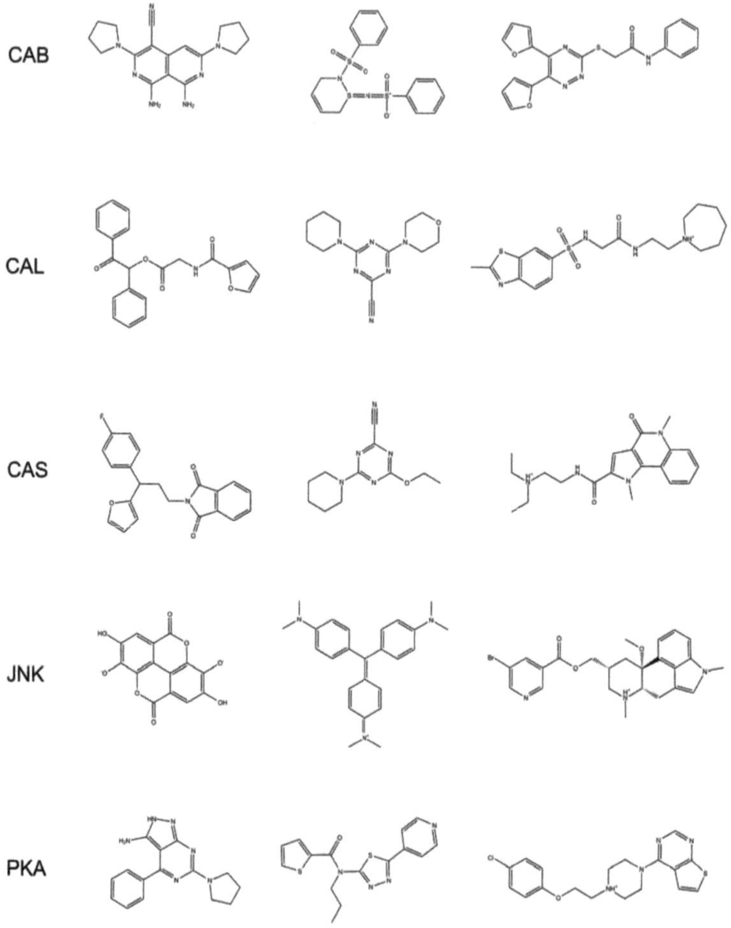

CAB

CAL

CAS

JNK

PKA

Fig. C.1: Representative active compounds.

Appendix D
Class-Unique ACCS Combinations

In Chapter 5 the distribution of ACCS in active and database compounds is analyzed. The detailed distribution of ACCS for the activity classes ARI and CAB is provided here.

Table D.1: ACCS distribution for ARI and CAB.

Reported are the number of active (N_{AC}) and ZINC database compounds (N_{DB}) that contain a certain number of ACCS (N_{ACCS}). No compound was found with more than 21 ARI-ACCS keys or 16 CAB-ACCS.

	ARI		CAB	
N_{ACCS}	N_{AC}	N_{DB}	N_{AC}	N_{DB}
0	2	3 238 820	0	3 097 965
1	1	280 284	6	166 257
2	3	125 760	5	326 925
3	2	18 465	3	69 484
4	1	3 016	3	13 293
5	0	2 996	2	3 613
6	2	10 166	2	2 259
7	1	1 406	0	963
8	1	1 073	3	513
9	1	208	2	185
10	2	1 226	4	82
11	1	833	0	847
12	2	67	1	899
13	1	39	1	963
14	2	57	2	139
15	1	11	1	51
16	0	3	1	5
17	0	0		
18	0	3		
19	0	8		
20	0	0		
21	0	2		

Tab. D.1: ACCS distribution for ARI and CAB.

Bibliography

[1] Merlot, C.; Domine, D.; Cleva, C.; Church, D. J. Chemical Substructures in Drug Discovery. *Drug Discov. Today* **2003**, *8*, 594-602.

[2] Bajorath, J. Selected Concepts and Investigations in Compound Classification, Molecular Descriptor Analysis, and Virtual Screening. *J. Chem. Inf. Comput. Sci.* **2001**, *41*, 233–245.

[3] Ertl, P.; Jelfs, S. Designing Drugs on the Internet? Free Web Tools and Services Supporting Medicinal Chemistry. *Curr. Top. Med. Chem.* **2007**, *7*, 1491–1501.

[4] Benson, S. W.; Buss, J. H. Additivity Rules for the Estimation of Molecular Properties. Thermodynamic Properties. *J. Chem. Phys.* **1958**, *29*, 546–572.

[5] Adamson, G. W.; Lynch, M. F.; Town, W. G. Analysis of Structural Characteristics of Chemical Compounds in a Large Computer-Based File. Part II. Atom-Centred Fragments. *J. Chem. Soc. C* **1971**, 3702–3706.

[6] Hiller, S. A.; Golender, V. E.; Rosenblit, A. B.; Rastrigin, L. A.; Glaz, A. B. Cybernetic Methods of Drug Design. I. Statement of the Problem–The Perceptron Approach. *Comput. Biomed. Res.* **1973**, *6*, 411–421.

[7] Hodes, L.; Hazard, G. F.; Geran, R. I.; Richman, S. A Statistical-Heuristic Method for Automated Selection of Drugs for Screening. *J. Med. Chem.* **1977**, *20*, 469–475.

[8] Willett, P. A Screen Set Generation Algorithm. *J. Chem. Inf. Comput. Sci.* **1979**, *19*, 159–162.

[9] Feldman, A.; Hodes, L. An Efficient Design for Chemical Structure Searching. I. The Screens. *J. Chem. Inf. Comput. Sci.* **1975**, *15*, 147–152.

[10] Morgan, H. L. The Generation of a Unique Machine Description for Chemical Structures-A Technique Developed at Chemical Abstracts Service. *J. Chem. Doc.* **1965**, *5*, 107–113.

[11] Adamson, G. W.; Cowell, J.; Lynch, M. F.; McLure, A. H. W.; Town, W. G.; Yapp, A. M. Strategic Considerations in the Design of a Screening System for Substructure Searches of Chemical Structure Files. *J. Chem. Doc.* **1973**, *13*, 153–157.

[12] Adamson, G. W.; Bush, J. A.; McLure, A. H. W.; Lynch, M. F. An Evaluation of a Substructure Search Screen System Based on Bond-Centered Fragments. *J. Chem. Doc.* **1974**, *14*, 44–48.

[13] Carhart, R.; Smith, D. H.; Venkataraghavan, R. Atom Pairs as Molecular Features in Structure-Activity Studies: Definition and Applications. *J. Chem. Inf. Comput. Sci.* **1985**, *25*, 64–73.

[14] Willett, P.; Winterman, V.; Bawden, D. Implementation of Nearest-Neighbor Searching in an Online Chemical Structure Search System. *J. Chem. Inf. Comput. Sci.* **1986**, *26*, 36–41.

[15] McGregor, M.; Pallai, P. Clustering of Large Databases of Compounds: Using the MDL "Keys" as Structural Descriptors. *J. Chem. Inf. Comput. Sci.* **1997**, *37*, 443–448.

[16] Barnard, J.; Downs, G. Chemical Fragment Generation and Clustering Software. *J. Chem. Inf. Comput. Sci.* **1997**, *37*, 141–142.

[17] Clark, M. Generalized Fragment-Substructure Based Property Prediction Method. *J. Chem. Inf. Model.* **2004**, *45*, 30–38.

[18] Matter, H.; Baringhaus, K. H.; Naumann, T.; Klabunde, T.; Pirard, B. Computational Approaches Towards the Rational Design of Drug-Like Compound Libraries. *Comb. Chem. High Throughput. Screen.* **2001**, *4*, 453–475.

[19] Oprea, T.; Davis, A.; Teague, S.; Leeson, P. Is There a Difference Between Leads and Drugs? A Historical Perspective. *J. Chem. Inf. Comput. Sci.* **2001**, *41*, 1308–1315.

[20] Patchett, A. A.; Nargund, R. P. Chapter 26. Privileged Structures – An Update. *Annu. Rep. Med. Chem.* **2000**, *35*, 289–298.

[21] Evans, B. E.; Rittle, K. E.; Bock, M. G.; DiPardo, R. M.; Freidinger, R. M.; Whitter, W. L.; Lundell, G. F.; Veber, D. F.; Anderson, P. S.; et al., Methods for Drug Discovery: Development of Potent, Selective, Orally Effective Cholecystokinin Antagonists. *J. Med. Chem.* **1988**, *31*, 2235–2246.

[22] Aronov, A. M.; McClain, B.; Moody, C. S.; Murcko, M. A. Kinase-Likeness and Kinase-Privileged Fragments: Toward Virtual Polypharmacology. *J. Med. Chem.* **2008**, *13*, 1214–1222.

[23] Aronov, A. M.; Bemis, G. W. A Minimalist Approach to Fragment-Based Ligand Design Using Common Rings and Linkers: Application to Kinase Inhibitors. *Proteins* **2004**, *57*, 36–50.

[24] Schnur, D.; Beno, B. R.; Good, A.; Tebben, A. Approaches to Target Class Combinatorial Library Design. *Methods Mol. Biol.* **2004**, *275*, 355–378.

[25] Tan, D. S. Diversity-Oriented Synthesis: Exploring the Intersections Between Chemistry and Biology. *Nat. Chem. Biol.* **2005**, *1*, 74–84.

[26] Bender, A.; Mussa, H. Y.; Glen, R. C.; Reiling, S. Similarity Searching of Chemical Databases Using Atom Environment Descriptors (MOLPRINT 2D): Evaluation of Performance. *J. Chem. Inf. Comput. Sci.* **2004**, *44*, 170–178.

[27] Xing, L.; Glen, R. Novel Methods for the Prediction of logP, pKa, and logD. *J. Chem. Inf. Comput. Sci.* **2002**, *42*, 796–805.

[28] Kearsley, S.; Sallamack, S.; Fluder, E.; Andose, J.; Mosley, R.; Sheridan, R. Chemical Similarity Using Physiochemical Property Descriptors. *J. Chem. Inf. Comput. Sci.* **1996**, *36*, 118–127.

[29] Bemis, G.; Murcko, M. The Properties of Known Drugs. 1. Molecular Frameworks. *J. Med. Chem.* **1996**, *39*, 2887–2893.

[30] Bemis, G.; Murcko, M. Properties of Known Drugs. 2. Side Chains. *J. Med. Chem.* **1999**, *42*, 5095–5099.

[31] Hajduk, P. J.; Greer, J. A Decade of Fragment-Based Drug Design: Strategic Advances and Lessons Learned. *Nat. Rev. Drug. Discov.* **2007**, *6*, 211–219.

[32] Schneider, G.; Fechner, U. Computer-Based De Novo Design of Drug-Like Molecules. *Nat. Rev. Drug. Discov.* **2005**, *4*, 649–663.

[33] Gillet, V.; Myatt, G.; Zsoldos, Z.; Johnson, P. SPROUT, HIPPO and CAESA: Tools for De Novo Structure Generation and Estimation of Synthetic Accessibility. *Perspect. Drug Discovery Des.* **1995**, *3*, 34–50.

[34] Lewell, X. Q.; Judd, D. B.; Watson, S. P.; Hann, M. M. RECAP-Retrosynthetic Combinatorial Analysis Procedure: A Powerful New Technique for Identifying Privileged Molecular Fragments with Useful Applications in Combinatorial Chemistry. *J. Chem. Inf. Comput. Sci.* **1998**, *38*, 511–522.

[35] Erlanson, D. A.; McDowell, R. S.; O'Brien, T. Fragment-Based Drug Discovery. *J. Med. Chem.* **2004**, *47*, 3463–3482.

[36] Durant, J. L.; Leland, B. A.; Henry, D. R.; Nourse, J. G. Reoptimization of MDL Keys for Use in Drug Discovery. *J. Chem. Inf. Comput. Sci.* **2002**, *42*, 1273–1280.

[37] Todeschini, R.; Consonni, V. *Handbook of Molecular Descriptors*, 1st ed.; Wiley-VCH, **2000**; Vol. 11.

[38] Xue, L.; Godden, J.; Gao, H.; Bajorath, J. Identification of a Preferred Set of Molecular Descriptors for Compound Classification Based on Principal Component Analysis. *J. Chem. Inf. Comput. Sci.* **1999**, *39*, 699–704.

[39] Bender, A.; Glen, R. A Discussion of Measures of Enrichment in Virtual Screening: Comparing the Information Content of Descriptors with Increasing Levels of Sophistication. *J. Chem. Inf. Model.* **2005**, *45*, 1369–1375.

[40] Matter, H. Selecting Optimally Diverse Compounds from Structure Databases: A Validation Study of Two-Dimensional and Three-Dimensional Molecular Descriptors. *J. Med. Chem.* **1997**, *40*, 1219–1229.

[41] Graham, D. J.; Malarkey, C.; Schulmerich, M. V. Information Content in Organic Molecules: Quantification and Statistical Structure via Brownian Processing. *J. Chem. Inf. Comput. Sci.* **2004**, *44*, 1601–1611.

[42] Graham, D.; Schulmerich, M. Information Content in Organic Molecules: Reaction Pathway Analysis via Brownian Processing. *J. Chem. Inf. Comput. Sci.* **2004**, *44*, 1612–1622.

[43] Graham, D. Information Content in Organic Molecules: Aggregation States and Solvent Effects. *J. Chem. Inf. Model.* **2005**, *45*, 1223–1236.

[44] Batista, J.; Godden, J.; Bajorath, J. Assessment of molecular similarity from the analysis of randomly generated structural fragment populations. *J. Chem. Inf. Comput. Sci.*, **2006** *46*, 1937–1944.

[45] Zemlyachenko, V. N.; Korneenko, N. M.; Tyshkevich, R. I. Graph Isomorphism Problem. *J. Math. Sci.* **1985**, *29*, 1426–1481.

[46] Fortin, S. The Graph Isomorphism Problem. *tech. report TR 96-20, Univer. of Alberta*, **1996**.

[47] Ullmann, J. R. An Algorithm for Subgraph Isomorphism. *J. ACM.* **1976**, *23*, 31–42.

[48] Bunke, H.; Foggia, P.; Guidobaldi, C.; Sansone, C.; Vento, M. A Comparison of Algorithms for Maximum Common Subgraph on Randomly Connected Graphs. In *Structural, Syntactic, and Statistical Pattern Recognition*; Lecture Notes in Computer Science; Springer, **2002**; pp 85–106.

[49] Dalby, A.; Nourse, J. G.; Hounshell, W. D.; Gushurst, A. K. I.; Grier, D. L.; Leland, B. A.; Laufer, J. A Comparison of Algorithms for Maximum Common Subgraph on Randomly Connected Graphs. *J. Chem. Inf. Comput. Sci.* **1992**, *32*, 244–255.

[50] Weininger, D. SMILES, a Chemical Language and Information System. 1. Introduction to Methodology and Encoding Rules. *J. Chem. Inf. Comput. Sci.* **1988**, *28*, 31–36.

[51] Batista, J.; Bajorath, J. Chemical database mining through entropy-based molecular similarity assessment of randomly generated structural fragment populations. *J. Chem. Inf. Model.*, **2007**, *47*, 59–68.

[52] Shannon, C. E. A Mathematical Theory of Communication. *Bell Syst. Technol. J.* **1948**, *27*, 379–423.

[53] Dancoff, S. M.; Quastler, H. The Information Content and Error Rate of Living Things. In *Information Theory in Biology*. Univer. of Illinois Press:Urbana, IL, **1953**.

[54] Bonchev, D.; Trinajstić, N. Information Theory, Distance Matrix, and Molecular Branching. *J. Chem. Phys.* **1977**, *67*, 4517–4533.

[55] Ho, M.; Vedene H. Smith, J.; Weaver, D. F.; Gatti, C.; Sagar, R. P.; Esquivel, R. O. Molecular Similarity Based on Information Entropies and Distances. *J. Chem. Phys.* **1998**, *108*, 5469–5475.

[56] Godden, J. W.; Stahura, F. L.; Bajorath, J. Variability of Molecular Descriptors in Compound Databases Revealed by Shannon Entropy Calculations. *J. Chem. Inf. Comput. Sci.* **2000**, *40*, 796–800.

[57] Wegner, J.; Frohlich, H.; Zell, A. Feature Selection for Descriptor Based Classification Models. 1. Theory and GA-SEC Algorithm. *J. Chem. Inf. Comput. Sci.* **2004**, *44*, 921–930.

[58] Godden, J.; Bajorath, J. Differential Shannon Entropy as a Sensitive Measure of Differences in Database Variability of Molecular Descriptors. *J. Chem. Inf. Comput. Sci.* **2001**, *41*, 1060–1066.

[59] Willett, P.; Barnard, J.; Downs, G. Chemical Similarity Searching. *J. Chem. Inf. Comput. Sci.* **1998**, *38*, 983–996.

[60] Bajorath, J. Integration of Virtual and High-Throughput Screening. *Nat. Rev. Drug. Discov.* **2002**, *1*, 882–894.

[61] Schneider, G.; Neidhart, W.; Giller, T.; Schmid, G. "Scaffold-Hopping" by Topological Pharmacophore Search: A Contribution to Virtual Screening. *Angew. Chem. Int. Ed.* **1999**, *38*, 2894–2896.

[62] *Concepts and Applications of Molecular Similarity*; Johnson, M. A., Maggiora, G. M., Eds.; Wiley:New York, NY, **1990**.

[63] Xue, L.; Bajorath, J. Accurate Partitioning of Compounds Belonging to Diverse Activity Classes. *J. Chem. Inf. Comput. Sci.* **2002**, *42*, 757–764.

[64] Xue, L.; Godden, J.; Stahura, F.; Bajorath, J. Mini-Fingerprints for Virtual Screening: Design Principles and Generation of Novel Prototypes Based on Information Theory. *J. Chem. Inf. Comput. Sci.* **2003**, *43*, 1151–1157.

[65] Schuffenhauer, A.; Floersheim, P.; Acklin, P.; Jacoby, E. Similarity Metrics for Ligands Reflecting the Similarity of the Target Proteins. *J. Chem. Inf. Comput. Sci.* **2003**, *43*, 391–405.

[66] Batista, J.; Bajorath, J. Mining of randomly generated molecular fragment populations uncovers activity-specific fragment hierarchies. *J. Chem. Inf. Model.*, **2007**, *47*, 1405–1413.

[67] Lounkine, E.; Batista, J.; Bajorath, J. Mapping of activity-specific fragment pathways isolated from random fragment populations reveals the formation of coherent molecular cores. *J. Chem. Inf. Model.*, **2007**, *47*, 2133–2139.

[68] Hert, J.; Willett, P.; Wilton, D.; Acklin, P.; Azzaoui, K.; Jacoby, E.; Schuffenhauer, A. Comparison of Fingerprint-Based Methods for Virtual Screening Using Multiple Bioactive Reference Structures. *J. Chem. Inf. Comput. Sci.* **2004**, *44*, 1177–1185.

[69] Tovar, A.; Eckert, H.; Bajorath, J. Comparison of 2D Fingerprint Methods for Multiple-Template Similarity Searching on Compound Activity Classes of Increasing Structural Diversity. *ChemMedChem* **2007**, *2*, 208–217.

[70] Batista, J.; Bajorath, J.; Distribution of randomly generated activity class characteristic substructures in diverse active and database compounds. *Mol. Divers.*, **2008**, *12*, 77–83.

[71] Gansner, E. R.; North, S. C. An Open Graph Visualization System and its Applications to Software Engineering. *Softw. Pract. Exper.* **2000**, *30*, 1203–1233.

[72] Irwin, J.; Shoichet, B. ZINC - A Free Database of Commercially Available Compounds for Virtual Screening. *J. Chem. Inf. Model.* **2005**, *45*, 177–182.

VDM Verlagsservicegesellschaft mbH

Die VDM Verlagsservicegesellschaft sucht für wissenschaftliche Verlage abgeschlossene und herausragende

Dissertationen, Habilitationen, Diplomarbeiten, Master Theses, Magisterarbeiten usw.

für die kostenlose Publikation als Fachbuch.

Sie verfügen über eine Arbeit, die hohen inhaltlichen und formalen Ansprüchen genügt, und haben Interesse an einer honorarvergüteten Publikation?

Dann senden Sie bitte erste Informationen über sich und Ihre Arbeit per Email an *info@vdm-vsg.de*.

Sie erhalten kurzfristig unser Feedback!

VDM Verlagsservicegesellschaft mbH
Dudweiler Landstr. 99
D - 66123 Saarbrücken

Telefon +49 681 3720 174
Fax +49 681 3720 1749

www.vdm-vsg.de

Die VDM Verlagsservicegesellschaft mbH vertritt

Printed by Books on Demand GmbH, Norderstedt / Germany